Managing Difficult Behaviour

A handbook for foster carers of the under 12s

Clare Pallett, Kathy Blackeby, William Yule,
Roger Weissman and Stephen Scott

with **Eileen Fursland**

BAAF
ADOPTION
& FOSTERING

Published by
British Association for Adoption & Fostering
(BAAF)
Saffron House
6–10 Kirby Street
London EC1N 8TS
www.baaf.org.uk

Charity registration 275689

British Library Cataloguing in Publication Data
A catalogue record for this book is available from the British Library

ISBN 978 1 905664 27 6

Project management by Shaila Shah, Director of Publications, BAAF
All cartoons by Fran Orford
Designed and typeset by Andrew Haig & Associates
Printed in Great Britain by The Lavenham Press
Trade distribution by Turnaround Publisher Services, Unit 3, Olympia Trading Estate,
Coburg Road, London N22 6TZ

BAAF is the leading UK-wide membership organisation for all those concerned with adoption, fostering and child care issues.

Contents

Notes about the authors

The Fostering Changes author team

Clare Pallett is employed by the South London and Maudsley Trust and was co-ordinator of the Fostering Changes Programme, providing skills-based training to foster carers in the London Borough of Southwark.

Kathy Blackeby was a social worker in the National Specialist Adoption and Fostering team at Maudsley Hospital for 11 years, during which time she developed and ran the foster care training course with colleagues. She is currently working as a child mental health specialist in London.

William Yule is a clinical psychologist and a Professor of Applied Child Psychology. He has worked since 1969 in a multi-disciplinary child mental health team that has a special interest in fostering and adoption issues.

Roger Weissman works as a child mental health social work team manager. He has wide experience of working with families and children in distress and experiencing relationship difficulties. He has taught on counselling and social work courses, and also worked with children with special needs. His particular professional interests include the emotional wellbeing of adopted children and those in the local authority care system.

Stephen Scott (BSc FRCP FRCPsychology) is Professor of Child Health and Behaviour, Institute of Psychiatry, King's College London and Director of Research, National Academy for Parenting Practitioners.

Freelance writer

Eileen Fursland is a professional freelance writer. She has written a number of books and feature stories for magazines, amongst them *Preparing to Adopt: A training pack for preparation groups* for BAAF (alongside a BAAF working party), *A Guide for Medical Advisers: Advocating, promoting and protecting the health of looked after children in Scotland* (with Ian Millar), *Trauma and Recovery: A training programme* and *Safer Caring: A training programme* (with Kate Cairns), all published by BAAF.

Cartoonist

Fran Orford's cartoons have been used in over 70 magazines and newspapers in both the UK and abroad, including *The Observer*, *Private Eye* and *The Telegraph*. Before becoming a cartoonist Fran set up and ran a Leaving Care Team for NCH in Halifax, West Yorkshire, and before that he worked with homeless and disadvantaged teenagers in London.

Acknowledgements

We would like to thank the foster carers from the London Borough of Southwark who have given their time and energy to attending the Fostering Changes Training Programme. We are grateful for their openness and their willingness to try out new ways of working with and relating to children in their care. Special thanks go to Stella, Colleen, Heather and Sally who generously shared their experiences of taking part in training and described the impact this had on the way they worked as carers. We would also like to thank the London Borough of Southwark Social Services Department, the South London and Maudsley Trust and Southwark Primary Care Trust for supporting and encouraging this work with foster carers.

Especial thanks and gratitude go to the various members of the Conduct, Adoption and Fostering Team at the Maudsley Hospital. They have worked hard to learn from academic research world-wide and to apply the findings to developing services that benefit children and their carers here in the UK. Their knowledge, experience and clinical practice has provided the fertile ground out of which the Fostering Changes programme has grown.

There are a whole host of colleagues and practitioners whose work in the field of parent training informed and inspired the development of the Fostering Changes Programme. In particular, we would like to thank Carolyn Webster-Stratton, The Centre for Fun and Families, Matt Sanders and the Triple P Positive Parenting Programme and Rex Forehand and Robert MacMahon. Special thanks go to Eileen Fursland who has taken the ideas and materials from the original *Fostering Changes* training programme and adapted these for direct use by foster carers.
She has done this with refreshing clarity, humour and directness.

Thank you to colleagues at Woodside Fostering for reading through an earlier draft of the script, and for their valuable comments. And finally, thanks to Fran Orford for his cartoons, which are both humorous and thought-provoking.

January 2008

A note about 'Fostering Changes: How to improve relationships and manage difficult behaviour'

Caring for looked after children can be an immensely stressful and complex task and foster carers need opportunities to process their experiences and reflect on their thoughts and feelings. The *Fostering Changes* Programme was set up in 1999 at the Maudsley Hospital, London, to provide practical advice and skills-based training for foster carers in order to develop their skills in managing difficult and challenging child behaviour and forming positive relationships with the children whom they look after.

This unique handbook, *Managing Difficult Behaviour*, has been developed from that training programme and is designed for use with foster carers in the local authority and voluntary and independent sectors. Many of the ideas and strategies are used in parent training programmes which use a cognitive behavioural approach to work with parents in order to develop their skills. The course has been evaluated and the evidence has shown significant improvements in carer–child interaction, specific child problems causing most worry to carers, and child emotional symptoms. It has also demonstrated a beneficial effect on carers' sense of confidence and self-efficacy.

By reading this handbook, foster carers will be able to acquaint themselves with some of the techniques suggested in the training programme, but reading the handbook on its own is not the same as actually attending a training course, in which the learning, group work, homework, skills practice and continuous evaluation result in a different experiential learning, which this handbook cannot entirely provide on its own. However, this handbook will give you a good flavour of the ideas and approaches used in training and provide clear guidance and advice on a number of different strategies to try out with the children in your care. These are designed to help you feel more calm and confident and to facilitate positive changes in the ways your child thinks, feels and behaves.

Is this programme for you?

As a foster carer, you are with your child every day and you are an important person in his life – so you are the one who can do most to help improve his behaviour and boost his self-esteem.

Here's some questions to ask yourself.

- Would you like to develop a better relationship with the child you are caring for? **Yes/No**
- Do you feel you are constantly nagging your child? **Yes/No**
- Do you sometimes struggle to deal with his tantrums, rudeness or aggression? **Yes/No**
- Do you sometimes wish you felt more warmly towards her? **Yes/No**
- Does he have a low opinion of himself? **Yes/No**
- Does she sometimes wind you up until you feel desperate or at the end of your tether? **Yes/No**
- Do you sometimes feel powerless when you want to get him to do something? **Yes/No**
- Do you often find things she does irritating or annoying? **Yes/No**
- Does he often play up to get your attention? **Yes/No**
- Does she seem to find it impossible to concentrate or get on with things on her own? **Yes/No**

If you answered "yes" to several (or all) of these questions, the training programme in this book is for you. It will give you new skills which will help you to improve your child's behaviour. The techniques and strategies you learn will help you achieve a more positive relationship with your child and a more harmonious family life. Learning to behave well will also make your child feel better about himself.

Developed by experts, tried and tested by carers

This book is based on a training programme for foster carers looking after children with challenging behaviour, called *Fostering Changes*. The training programme was set up in 1999 at the Maudsley Hospital, London, by a group of experienced clinicians in adoption and fostering and child psychology and psychiatry. It is now a standard part of training for new carers in Southwark (in London), and has also been used elsewhere with success.

The training programme is based on the well-established principles of social learning theory, and targets patterns of behaving, relating and thinking. Parenting training programmes based on these techniques, delivered in a structured way over several weeks, have been found to be the single most effective way of treating behaviour problems in children.

The results of the *Fostering Changes* training programme have been outstanding.

Many of the carers who have completed the programme are delighted with the changes they have managed to make. The evidence has shown significant improvements in the interactions between carers and children as well as in the children's problem behaviours and emotional symptoms. Learning the new skills also helped carers feel more confident and competent.

> **'Life is so much better for all of us'**
>
> **Sally had been fostering six-year-old twins, a boy and a girl, for nine months when she went on the Fostering Changes course.**
>
> *'Charlie had very challenging behaviour. He was aggressive, would lash out, smash up his room and destroy things. He would do this not only at times when he was angry or anxious but just out of the blue – he would snap a pair of sunglasses, for instance, or run something under the tap to spoil it. He had no sense of danger and would dash out into the road and run up and down the aisles in the supermarket.*
>
> *'Rosie was very guarded and would become very tearful at the slightest thing. She would say that she hated herself, that she's not a nice person. Even something as small as my saying it was too late for a bedtime story would be enough to start the tears and she would say distressing things like: "I wish I was dead".*
>
> *'But the strategies I learned on the course certainly worked for these two. I was surprised at the effect it has had.'*
>
> *Charlie's behaviour had been a big issue but once Sally had learned how to manage it, everything changed – and she felt able to adopt the twins.*
>
> *'Charlie's behaviour has gone from being the worst you could think of to just really occasional instances. Children can be as adorable as you like, but their challenging behaviour could make you think: "I can't handle that" – which would have been such a shame for Charlie and Rosie. Since going on the course, life for all of us has been so much better.'*

The White Paper, *Care Matters* (2007), states that the Government plans to roll out the *Fostering Changes* programme to agencies as part of a national programme.

Learn how to help your child behave well

If you can take part in a *Fostering Changes* training programme, this book will act as a reminder and back-up for you once the course is over. If you can't attend the training in person, this book will allow you to work through much of the programme at home on your own. It explains the techniques and strategies and provides training exercises which will help you to develop a range of skills in managing behaviour.

Being a good foster carer demands many of the same qualities as being a good parent, but of course there are big differences: you are working in a different context, with children with very different needs. However, the social learning techniques and strategies in this book can be used in any family situation and with all children. They are consistent with the positive approach to discipline that fostering agencies advocate.

The programme set out in the book won't provide you with all the answers – there are no "right answers" when dealing with the infinite variety of ways that troubled children express their frustration, anger, stress and insecurity. But it will provide you with ways in which you can help your child, in your own way, in your own home.

These techniques and strategies are not difficult to understand or to put into practice. They will help you to build positive bonds with your child and to encourage good behaviour, set limits and apply discipline. The improvements in your relationship and in your child's behaviour will make every day easier and more enjoyable not only for him, but also for you and the rest of your family.

And in the long term, helping your child learn to behave more appropriately could transform his life.

'It was really helpful'

Heather was fostering a three-year-old girl with severe behaviour problems.

'As a foster carer, you go on lots of courses and although you hope they will be useful you often think, "It's just another course". But the Fostering Changes *course was really helpful. Her problem behaviour didn't stop altogether but in the end she changed.'*

Looking at behaviour

Looked after children are a diverse group, with a great variety of needs. These children have widely different social, ethnic and religious backgrounds, and diverse experiences of family and community life, and all of these factors must be considered by the social workers and foster carers looking after them. But one common point is that many of these children will have been damaged by their early life experiences and may consequently have high levels of social, physical, educational and mental health difficulties; fostering them is therefore a complex, stressful task. These children may be depressed, anxious, chronically lacking in confidence, and have poor social skills. They may also behave aggressively, be withdrawn, destructive, impulsive and out of control. Children presenting such behaviours can represent a challenge even for the most dedicated, skilled and experienced foster carers.

Sometimes, children's problems are not so serious, yet daily life with them can still be wearing because they demand constant attention or reassurance or have developed irritating, antisocial habits.

Which behaviour would you like to tackle?

The first step in tackling difficult behaviour is to be clear about what the child is actually doing. It's easy to say something sweeping, like 'He's lazy' or 'She's disobedient'. But in order to change things, you need to be more precise. For example: 'He lies on the sofa and watches television while the rest of us are clearing up after supper' or 'When I tell her to stop doing something, she ignores me'.

If you can identify the behaviour quite precisely, it is easier to decide the best way to change it. It's also easier to recognise improvements when they occur. This programme will introduce you to a number of different strategies you can use to change your child's behaviour.

Rate the three main problems

What are your main concerns about the child you are looking after? List the three problem behaviours that you would most like to reduce.

Problem 1: _____

Not a problem ◄—————————————————————————► Couldn't be worse

Problem 2: _____

Not a problem ◄—————————————————————————► Couldn't be worse

Problem 3: _____

Not a problem ◄—————————————————————————► Couldn't be worse

If you are willing to work through the exercises in each chapter of this book, think about what you have learned and put it into practice with determination and perseverance, you will soon have several new and effective ways to tackle these and other problems.

Reference

Department for Education and Skills (2007) *Care Matters: Time for change*, London: The Stationery Office

1 Why do children behave the way they do?

In response to the way adults in their lives treat them, children develop certain ways of behaving and relating to people and certain beliefs and feelings about themselves.

So when a child comes to you and some of the things she does and says surprise you, you need to think about how she might have learned these things in the first place.

Many children coming into foster care have experienced serious physical and/ or emotional abuse or neglect, loss and trauma. Many of them have mental health problems or behaviour disorders. Because of the difficult start they have had or the way adults in their lives have treated them, many of these children either "can't behave" or "won't behave". In other words, they have developed behaviour patterns which allowed them to survive in a situation of neglect or abuse, but which are not appropriate in normal family life, school and other social situations.

The ABC of behaviour: a model for understanding how behaviour is learned

Most behaviour is learned – which means it is shaped by our environment, in particular by our interactions with other people. Other people's responses can make it more or less likely that we will behave in a particular way.

For example, if you go out of your way to cook a nice meal for a friend and the friend is genuinely enthusiastic and appreciative, you will probably want to do it again another time. If, on the other hand, the friend takes your efforts for granted, you will be less inclined to bother again.

The A B C model

The A B C model provides a simple way of thinking about behaviour:

A is the antecedent or trigger which comes before the behaviour

B is the behaviour

C is the consequence, or what comes after the behaviour.

A → B ← → C

Behaviour is influenced both by what comes before it – its antecedent or trigger – and by its consequences. So it may be possible to change the antecedents and the consequences in order to produce changes in behaviour.

Antecedents or triggers

Antecedents or triggers occur immediately before the behaviour. They might be to do with when, where and with whom the particular behaviour occurs. For example:

- A **place**, a particular **person** or **situation** can act as a trigger. For example, your child might be prone to tantrums at the supermarket checkout when she can see sweets on display; or she might be emotionally volatile when she is about to have a visit to her birth family or has just returned from seeing them; or bedtime might be the trigger time for crying or playing up.

- **Social cues** – such as criticism or even just a look or tone of voice that the child perceives as hostile – can trigger a response.

- **Copying** – children copy both appropriate and inappropriate behaviour; for instance, they may copy something they have seen someone do on television or the behaviour of other children in school.

- **Triggers from the past.** The easiest triggers to understand are those that occur in the present, but sometimes memories from the past can act as a trigger. For instance, a child who was abused at bathtime may respond with fear or aggression when her carer tells her to have a bath. The memory of the abuse evokes unpleasant thoughts and feelings, which then affect the way the child behaves. Foster carers are, of course, not always aware of children's past experiences so sometimes find it hard to understand their behaviour.

- **Self-talk.** We all have certain beliefs about ourselves and the world. A child who has negative beliefs about herself, for instance, because she has been told that she is stupid or clumsy, may try to avoid or withdraw from situations which trigger her fear of failure. Like triggers from the past, these negative beliefs are not always obvious to other people.

Other factors that play a part

There are other factors in children's lives which, while they are not immediate triggers, do affect their behaviour. For instance, poor health, medication, a poor diet, lack of sleep, uncertainty about the future and so on can all affect the way a child reacts and responds to everyday situations.

A pay-off encourages the behaviour

When we do something and the consequence is positive or rewarding, we are more likely to repeat the behaviour. The reward or "pay-off" can come in many different forms, including praise and attention.

To strengthen a particular behaviour in a child, you need to reward it consistently and reliably, for instance, by praising the child every time she tidies her bedroom or takes her dirty plate to the kitchen. Once the behaviour has become established, occasional praise will be enough to keep it up.

But if the consequence is negative or unpleasant, this makes us less likely to repeat the behaviour.

Be careful not to reward inappropriate behaviour

We create problems when we unwittingly provide pay-offs for behaviour we do not want to encourage. Attention from a carer is a powerful motivator for a child, so we need to use it carefully.

It may seem hard to understand, but some children are so hungry for attention that they would rather have a telling-off than no attention at all.

One of the problems in family life is when carers fail to reward good behaviour and inadvertently reward bad behaviour. For example, if a carer leaves a child alone and ignores her whenever she plays quietly, over time this behaviour may fade away because it is not bringing the child any rewards in terms of the carer's attention. But if the carer always takes notice of her – even with a telling-off – when she fights or argues or throws things around, this gets her the attention she wants. The attention rewards the behaviour and makes her more likely to argue, fight and throw things around again in the future.

Avoiding something unpleasant is a pay-off too

Suppose a child does not want to go to school because she is trying to avoid taking a test or is being bullied, so she cries and complains of a stomach-ache. If the carer allows her to stay off school, she is rewarding the behaviour – because the pay-off is that the child gets to avoid taking the test or confronting the bullies in the playground.

When one thing leads to another

Problem behaviours like tantrums and destructiveness are not in fact single, isolated behaviours but are a kind of chain of behaviours that often follow a pattern. One thing leads to another, and often the explosion can spring from something quite small.

Take this example of a typical supermarket tantrum:

1 **Child sees sweets on the shelf**
2 **Asks for sweets**
3 **Picks them up and won't let go**
4 **Starts shouting**
5 **Cries**
6 **Kicks**
7 **Runs away from carer, clutching sweets**

In the early stages of this process the child may still be open to reason, firmness or distraction. But once the behaviour has escalated beyond a certain point, it's very hard to stop it. You get tense and annoyed yourself and may also start shouting. This actually makes the child's tantrum even worse. One of the following scenarios usually follows:

1 **Carer gives in and buys the sweets, in desperation or anger. Child learns that behaving badly will get her what she wants.**

2 **Furious carer grabs child and storms out of supermarket. Child gets message that to get people to do what you want, you use threats, force and intimidation.**

Of course we are all only human and scenes like this can happen in most families at times, despite our best intentions. But it's better to break the vicious circle before things get out of control on both sides.

You might not be able to stop all the tantrums, all the time – but the way you respond when trouble is brewing can certainly make a big difference to the child's behaviour.

HOW?

- Be clear and consistent about your intentions - being vague, irritated or inconsistent will probably make the child behave even more badly.

- Keep your cool!

- Use distraction whenever you can - get the child to think about something else. Prevent a full-blown tantrum by distracting the child at an early stage of the process. For example, ask her to come and choose a dessert or breakfast cereal, or to choose a new toothbrush for herself.

Removing the trigger

The two brothers Claudia was fostering were taken to school by cab. She and the boys would sit in the back. Claudia would sit Peter in the middle because he was the youngest. But the boys would constantly fight in the back of the cab on the way to and from school.

Thinking about the problem, Claudia realised that one of the triggers for the fights was the boys sitting next to each other and winding each other up. So instead, she sat in the middle between them every day. Problem solved!

Claudia says: 'Some of the strategies are so simple, you think: Why didn't I think of that before?'

OVER TO YOU

Triggers and payoffs

Over the course of the next couple of days, explore how your child's behaviour is influenced by what happens before a particular behaviour and what happens afterwards. Try to notice the triggers for certain behaviours and the pay-offs for the child. Here are some examples:

- You ask your child to tidy her room – this is the trigger.
  Your child tidies her room. The pay-off is that you are pleased with her and give her some attention and praise.

- Your child didn't sleep well last night which means she is tired and irritable.
  You take her shopping with you and she has a tantrum because you won't buy her sweets. The trigger is the sight of the sweets in the shop. If you give in and buy them, you are providing a pay-off for the tantrum and making it more likely that it will happen again next time. If you keep your cool and refuse to buy the sweets, it will make a tantrum a little less likely next time.

- You tell the child she can watch television when she has done her homework.
  She argues and complains – which you ignore – but does her homework anyway. The pay-off is that she gets to watch television.

- Your child sees you cooking – this is the trigger – and wants to help.
  You both enjoy the time you spend together, preparing the meal. This – and the family's praise for the meal – are the pay-offs.

- Your child steals a bar of chocolate from the shop.
  She does not get caught. The pay-offs are getting chocolate for nothing and feeling smarter than adults – it makes her more likely to repeat the behaviour in future.

- She steals a bar of chocolate from the shop.
  You catch her doing it and make her give it back and apologise. As a consequence, she is not allowed to go out and play or watch any television that evening. This makes it less likely that she will repeat the behaviour in future.

Make a note of some of the behaviours you observe in your child over the next couple of days, with their triggers and pay-offs.

Remember that observing helps us to get a clearer picture and to see things in context. It also helps us to have a more objective record of what actually happens. And recording it will help you look back, reflect and see if and when things changed.

BEHAVIOUR	WHAT TRIGGERED IT?	WHAT WAS THE PAY-OFF, IF ANY?	COMMENT

2 How to be good at giving praise

Most children respond well to praise, encouragement and positive attention. In many children, these alone are enough to help them behave well. They are the foundation of a warm, positive relationship with carers. And without this kind of relationship, it is hard to exert any kind of discipline.

In this and the following two chapters, we will be looking at some of the main things you can use to encourage positive skills and behaviours in a child: praise, positive attention and tangible rewards.

Focus on the positive

Some children are so difficult that it's all too easy to get preoccupied with their problem behaviour. If you can't improve the way they behave, you can become demoralised and feel that you spend all your time nagging them or telling them off. The child feels he can't do anything right and the atmosphere at home becomes increasingly negative and tense. You end up having to punish him frequently for bad behaviour and things get even worse.

The trick is to break this negative cycle. You need to start to focus on the positive things the child does – however few and far between – and provide praise and encouragement for those. Many looked after children have experienced nothing but negative responses. If you can start to look out for the child's positive actions and qualities, it will help you as well as him. You will stop focusing on the problems and both you and the child will start to feel better. Your warmth, praise and positive attitude will make for a better relationship between you. Because of this relationship, the child will want to behave well to please you.

Rewarding with praise

Praise is an important way of providing a reward for positive behaviour. It shows the child that you have noticed he is behaving well.

Praise can be a smile, a pat on the back or a thumbs-up as well as words.

When children are quietly playing or getting on with what they are meant to be doing, often carers don't think to praise them. But if good behaviour goes unnoticed, the child may be more likely to start misbehaving in order to get attention.

- Use praise to provide positive attention for behaviour you want to encourage.

- Do not give any attention to minor inappropriate behaviour, where possible; in other words, ignore behaviour you want to discourage. This applies particularly to behaviour that is aimed at gaining your negative attention.

He never does anything I can praise him for!

Some children's behaviour is so poor that it can be hard to find anything to be pleased about. With these children, you have to make a conscious effort to "catch them being good" so you can give them some praise. Or you can set up situations or make requests that you are reasonably sure they will comply with – like 'please could you bring in the biscuits from the kitchen?' That way, the child can have the experience of being co-operative and pleasing you and being praised for this.

You can also praise children for not doing the things they usually do – for instance, 'Kirsty, you've had no fights tonight. I've really enjoyed being with you and your brothers. Well done!'

How do you feel about praise?

Sometimes, our own feelings and attitudes can get in the way of our being good at giving praise to children. Our own childhood experiences of being praised – or not – can affect the way we feel about giving praise. For instance:

- Some people feel unnatural or awkward giving praise.
- Some believe we should praise children only for exceptionally good behaviour or achievements.
- Some believe that praise will somehow spoil the child or go to their head.

Praising doesn't come easily to everyone and we need to practise.

Think about how you use praise with the children you look after. Are you sparing with your praise or do you provide lots of warm, enthusiastic, positive messages?

Some children find praise hard to take. They may have a very negative image of themselves and cannot accept warmth and encouragement.

Praise can be surprisingly powerful in motivating a child. It helps them to feel more positive about themselves and encourages good behaviour.

Sometimes carers feel unappreciated and don't get the praise they deserve. To practise your skills in praising, start by praising yourself. Here are some positive thoughts to get you started. Finish the sentences we have started.

Now add two more positive thoughts about yourself. You can do it!

Praise yourself!

I am a good carer because _____

My best qualities are _____

I am proud of the way I _____

I have helped my child by _____

Remember, carers need to value themselves if they are to be positive role models for the children in their care. So don't be afraid of praising yourself!

Self-praise is a valuable skill for children to develop – it can help them feel more positive about themselves. By praising yourself out loud in front of him, you are showing him how it's done.

Praising: how to make the most of it

You can use praise as a reward to encourage behaviour you would like to see more of. For instance, if you know that your child tends to be quite rough when playing with younger children, you can make a point of praising him whenever he plays nicely with them.

Praise works best when it is:

● **Specific, rather than vague or general.** If you say 'Good girl!' or 'Well done!', the child may not be clear about what it is they have actually done. Effective praise spells it out: 'I'm really pleased you are trying so hard to work through your maths homework', or 'Thank you for doing as I asked straight away'. This extra information helps looked after children to learn what is expected of them.

● **Sincere.** Praise delivered without any enthusiasm or eye contact is not as rewarding. So think about all the non-verbal aspects of your praise: the way you stop what you are doing and:
  – make eye contact;
  – the warmth and energy in your voice;
  – your touch; and
  – your smile.
  Even if this doesn't feel very natural to you at first, you can practise it and learn to express yourself in this way.

● **Immediate.** Praise works best when it comes straight after the positive behaviour. That way, the child can make the link between the behaviour and the reward. If you are trying to encourage a behaviour that doesn't happen very often, you need to look out for it and give lots of praise as soon as you notice the child doing it. It is important to praise the child as soon as he starts doing something – such as tidying away his toys – rather than waiting until he has finished and everything is put away. Praising him while he is tidying is encouraging for him and shows him that you have noticed and are pleased.

● **Appropriate.** Don't praise a child for playing with his little sister if, in fact, he is pulling faces and teasing her. Children need to be clear about what behaviour you want to see.

What to praise?

Here are some of the behaviours some carers have chosen to praise:

● Playing co-operatively with other children

● Eating a meal without messing around

● Speaking in a calm voice rather than shouting

● Saying please and thank you

● Doing as he is told the first time

Don't dilute praise with criticism

Praise should never be combined with a "put-down" – such as 'Well done for finishing your homework, but you really could have done it more neatly' or 'I'm pleased you've tidied your room – what a shame it took you three days to do it'. This spoils the effect of the praise and can be demotivating for the child, who may hold on to the negative message.

Praise small steps

If you want your child to learn how to dress himself, you might need to start by praising every little thing he does, like picking up a sock and putting it half-on his foot. Praise him for these small steps and it will encourage him to try out more.

Praise him for trying

If your child tries to do something you want him to do, praise him for his efforts even if he doesn't quite manage it.

Spontaneous praise and targeted praise

Spontaneous praise is the kind of praise you give, at any time, for good behaviour. Targeted praise is used when you have identified a problem behaviour, and you

OVER TO YOU

Practise your praising skills

Over the next couple of days, look for any opportunity to praise your child when you notice him behaving well. If it helps, jot down some ideas below. Remember to praise your child by simply describing the behaviour that you like. Here's a sample praise chart.

Day	Spontaneous praise 5x day	Targeted praise	Observations: what I said, what happened
Mon	✓✓ ✓✓	✓✓	Gary offered some sweets to Ben. Told him he was a kind boy to share. Praised him for saying goodnight to Ben.
Tues	✓✓ ✓✓		Difficult day – Gary in trouble at school. I was cross and disappointed – found it hard to praise. Gary was sullen.
Weds	✓✓✓ ✓✓ ✓✓	✓✓✓	I tried hard to look for positives today. Gary responded well. Played for over an hour without fighting.

then praise the child for the opposite and desired behaviour ("target behaviour"), whenever it occurs. So, you could think of a behaviour that you want to see instead of a problem behaviour, for example, talking quietly or politely instead of shouting, and then praising the appropriate behaviour whenever it occurs.

Turn around a difficult day

On one of those bad days when your child is playing up and you both feel ratty, try to find something, anything, to praise him for. You might just find saying something positive breaks the negative cycle, changes the mood and leaves you both feeling better.

Practise your praising skills

Over the next couple of days, look for any opportunity to praise your child when you notice him behaving well. If it helps, jot down some ideas below. Remember to praise your child by simply describing the behaviour that you like.

Some things I could praise my child for:

A good way to give praise is to tell the child how the behaviour makes you feel. Try jotting some specific things down.

There's no limit to the ways you can praise

I like it when you	_____
It helps me when you	_____
I'm so pleased that you	_____
You've done a great job of	_____

It is good to be descriptive in your praise. For example, 'You have used lots of beautiful bright colours in your painting' shows you have really bothered to notice what the child has done. This will mean more to the child than a more general comment like 'Fantastic picture!'

You could also praise the child indirectly by telling other people – in his presence – how good he is or how well he has done something.

Be generous with your praise!

'It worked for us'

Claudia fostered two brothers aged eight and six. She attended the Fostering Changes course to help her manage their challenging behaviour.

'I had always used praise but I learned I had to use a lot more. I learned creative ways of praising rather than just always saying "Well done". It helped them feel good about what they had done and I found it was less draining for me.

'Life is so hectic and busy when you are fostering that you don't have time to think. Sometimes you get caught up in noticing the unwanted behaviours and a lot of the good behaviour passes you by. There are lots of little things you don't always have time to notice. There were sometimes quite subtle things the younger boy was doing, like being kind to someone else and sharing things, and with all the day-to-day challenges I didn't always pick up on good behaviour like this. But once I started to praise these things, I could see his whole body language change and his pleasure was obvious.'

3 Using play to give positive attention

Many looked after children have learned, early on in their young lives, that the only way they will get any attention is by behaving badly. In their experience, they are ignored when they are quiet but they get attention – even if it's someone shouting at them – when they misbehave. And surprising as it may seem, children would rather have negative attention than none at all.

When a child comes to you, your task is to establish the opposite pattern. You need to make sure that you target your positive attention on her when she is behaving well, and pay her as little attention as possible when she is behaving inappropriately.

Most children love it when adults are interested in them and what they are doing. One of the skills that you need to develop as a carer is to actively take notice of the child when she is being good. Paying attention to her at these times will encourage and reward her for behaving well.

This chapter explains a strategy called "attending", which is a non-threatening way of getting alongside a child and positively supporting her while she is playing. It is a way of relating to a child that involves noticing what she is doing and showing interest. You don't try to show or tell her what to do or ask questions – you simply follow her lead.

"Attending" can be a powerful tool, especially for children who are not used to getting much positive attention from adults. If you can do it regularly, you and the child will probably start to feel much closer. It builds up trust between you and the child, and encourages her to feel more positive about herself. You may even find that her concentration improves and she can spend more time playing, even when you are not with her.

Just 10 minutes a day can make a big difference.

How to "attend"

The good news is that, for "attending", you only need to set aside 10 minutes a day. But that 10 minutes is a special time during which you have to give your full attention to the child.

This is what you do!

- **Follow the child's lead.** Follow her ideas and imagination rather than suggesting your own. That way, she will get more absorbed in the game and it helps her come up with more ideas. If she wants you to put all the cows in the dolls' house, don't question her logic – just do it!

- **Imitate what she does.** For instance, if she pushes a car along the floor, you might do the same. Mirror her actions without dominating.

- **Go at the child's pace.** Children often like to repeat activities until they feel they have entirely mastered them. This might seem boring to adults. But resist the temptation to speed things up by introducing new ideas and activities – that could just put her under pressure to "perform".

- **Be sensitive to the child.** Play does not need to have an aim or a goal – let the child do what she wants to do and wait for her to move on to another activity when she feels like it.

- **Avoid power struggles.** Play is one area where children can find out what it feels like to exercise power and control. This can help develop their sense of competence and independence. So be careful not to do anything that might undermine her – if you are building towers, don't build one that is better than hers! Remember, you want her to experience success.

- **Encourage her creativity.** It is the process of playing and experimenting that matters, not the finished product. So try not to suggest ways she could improve her picture, model or game, even if you can see how much better it could be! Praise her for her inventiveness, persistence and concentration.

- **Encourage imaginative play.** Pretending, dressing up and acting out stories with dolls or toy animals develops children's imagination. This kind of play helps them to experiment with different roles and think about other people's feelings. Imaginative play is a good opportunity for you to "attend" and enter into the fantasy world your child is creating.

- **Be an appreciative audience.** Keep focusing on the child – don't get so absorbed in your own play activity that you forget to enjoy what she is doing.

- **Laugh and have fun together!**

What to watch out for

Remember, while you are attending, resist the temptation to:

- ask questions

- take charge

- give instructions

- teach the child.

When an adult 'attends', a child feels special. Most children love the times when their carer is attending.

● ● ● ● ● ● ● ●

The right kind of play

When you have set aside time for attending, suggest three or four suitable toys, games or activities that lend themselves to creativity and imagination and let your child choose one. Alternatively, look out for a time when she is playing with something suitable – then drop everything for ten minutes so you can give her some positive attention.

Board games are not ideal for attending, because they are competitive and highly structured. It's also hard to attend while your child plays computer games so try to avoid these too. It would be best if your child is playing with bricks, cars, dolls, Lego, crayons or paints, etc.

Descriptive commenting

Many of us are used to asking lots of questions when we play with children: 'What's that you are drawing?'; 'Do you know what colour pigs are?' Although the aim is to help the child to learn, questions can be distracting for her. They interrupt her play and introduce the adult's agenda.

Another way of talking to the child while she plays is to use something called "descriptive commenting". You describe what the child is doing, almost like giving a running commentary. For instance: 'You are putting all the red cars together.

You're making the yellow car speed along…Now it's stopped…' Try to avoid tagging questions on to the end, like 'You've put them in the garage, haven't you?'

Your comments are like a flow of positive attention, keeping the child focused on what she is doing. A steady level of descriptive commenting can be particularly helpful for children who find it hard to concentrate.

Attending: how to do it well

You can use attending in short bursts at any time through the day. Times when your child is playing or drawing are good for attending but there are plenty of other opportunities. Show the child you have noticed what she is doing by describing and commenting on small things, like how she is cleaning out her hamster cage or doing her homework.

Attending is something we do quite naturally with babies – when we use baby-talk, we describe or mirror what the baby is doing. It feels intimate, warm and rewarding for both the adult and the baby. Attending is a way of doing something similar with older children.

Attending may feel odd at first. You have to break the habit of asking questions, teaching her things or suggesting what she should do. While you are attending, you let your child take the lead and engage with her in a more responsive, creative way. You can save the teaching and instructing for other times.

If your child seems puzzled when you first start attending, just explain that you are interested in what she is doing.

Ignore any minor misbehaviour while you are attending, if you can. Turn away from her and do something else until she has started behaving properly again. Do your best to make sure she can carry on playing. But if she starts doing something seriously aggressive or destructive, you may need to put a temporary stop to things. You might say: 'Because you are scratching the table, we will have to stop playing for a few minutes'.

Sometimes it can get boring when your child wants to play the same game or do the same thing over and over again. But attending only needs to last about 10 minutes each time – and it's important to use that short period of time to fully focus on the child and what she wants to do.

A word of warning – your child may enjoy it so much when you attend that she won't want you to stop. So give her a couple of minutes' notice that you will soon have to leave her to go and get on with your work or make a phone call – but reassure her that you will play again later or tomorrow.

Positive attention means more than any high-tech game. Many families fall into the trap of buying lots of expensive toys, computers and games consoles for children and expecting them to keep themselves amused. But actively joining in with the child when she's playing something simple is much more valuable.

Attending: key points

- Creative, open-ended and imaginative games work best
- Sit close to the child
- Follow and imitate the child's behaviour
- Notice it and describe it
- Make positive comments
- Let the child use her imagination
- Ignore minor misbehaviour
- Give a minute's warning before stopping
- Enjoy yourselves

Just try it out and see what happens! You won't necessarily see the benefits the first few times you do it, so keep at it. Many carers have been amazed at the changes in their children's behaviour after they have started attending regularly.

OVER TO YOU

Try attending for 10 minutes a day this week while your child is playing. If it helps, make notes here.

Notes about attending

DAY AND TIME	ACTIVITY	HOW I FELT ABOUT IT	HOW THE CHILD RESPONDED	OTHER COMMENTS
DAY 1				
DAY 2				
DAY 3				
DAY 4				
DAY 5				
DAY 6				
DAY 7				

'Attending has really helped'

At first Sally, foster carer to six-year-old twins Charlie and Rosie, wasn't convinced about attending.

'Sometimes you would think it's not going to work – but gosh, it did,' she says. 'You have to give it a go and keep at it, and the results can be quite surprising.'

Sally generally attends with Charlie while he is playing with toy aeroplanes and cars or sometimes he will choose a game.

'Charlie is not into drawing but Rosie loves anything like that. She likes playing with dolls and little toys that she moves around. At first it felt a bit awkward but after a while you get used to it and it feels natural.

'When Charlie is really attention-seeking, Rosie can feel left out. But now, with attending, they wait for my sole attention – they tell each other "It'll be your turn in a minute!"

'Together with the other strategies, attending has really worked.'

4 Using rewards

KEEP REWARDS SIMPLE

Praise and attention can really help a child to behave well, as we saw in Chapters 2 and 3. They act as a kind of social reward.

But sometimes praise and attention on their own are not enough. And there are a few children who don't respond particularly well to social rewards like these.

So for times when you need something extra, you can use more tangible or concrete rewards. These might include treats, small presents, pocket money or special privileges such as being allowed to stay up late.

Using tangible rewards like this is a short-term strategy – over a longer period, the social rewards will be more important for most children.

Giving rewards

There are three ways you can give rewards:

1 **You can give rewards out of the blue** – for instance, when you give your child a surprise treat when he has been behaving well or has done something particularly good.

2 **You can plan it in advance** so that he knows that if he completes a task or behaves in a particular way, you will give him a reward.

3 **You can use a reward chart** – see pages **37–41**.

You can use rewards for:

● Helping your child to behave better and be more co-operative

● Getting rid of particular problem behaviour such as shouting or getting out of bed at night

● Encouraging your child to learn a new skill such as cleaning his teeth or getting dressed by himself

● Getting him to do certain tasks such as homework or tidying his room

● Breaking habits such as night-time wetting

What motivates your child?

Think about what your child likes doing. You will know how he chooses to spend his time, what he gets excited about and what special times or activities he looks forward to. This will give you some ideas about what you could use as rewards.

Ask your child what he likes as well – you might be surprised by some of the things he comes up with!

Make a note of them in the box opposite.

The "when…then…" rule

Rewards should always be given *after* the child has done whatever it is you want him to do, not before. For instance: 'When you have finished your homework, then you can play on the computer' or 'When you have tidied your room, then we can go to the park'.

A reward every time?

When a child is learning to do something new, you should reward him every time he does it – whether you are using social rewards such as praise and a pat on the back, or a more tangible reward.

Later, when he has mastered it, you don't need to reward him every time – just occasionally. This will motivate him to continue the behaviour he has learned.

What my child likes

Food _____

Sweets/snacks _____

Favourite place _____

Favourite game _____

Activity _____

Favourite person _____

Special toy _____

Treats _____

Things he looks forward to _____

Things that cheer him up _____

Special times _____

Small gifts he would like _____

Any other ideas _____

How to make rewards work

For rewards to be really effective, they need to work in certain ways. They should be:

- **Specific**

  This means being clear about what the reward will be. Saying: 'We will do something nice' is not as effective as explaining 'I will read you a story' or 'We will have chocolate biscuits'.

- **Immediate**

  The reward should be given immediately after the behaviour you are trying to encourage. The longer the delay, the less effective the reward will be.

  Young children and children with poor concentration find it difficult to learn about the consequences of their behaviour. You have a better chance of success if you can give rewards often and straight after the behaviour – a smiley face sticker given immediately afterwards, every time, is better than a promise to buy him a treat next time you go shopping.

- **Consistent**

  Try to give rewards reliably and consistently. It is important that you notice good and appropriate behaviour and follow through with the rewards you have agreed.

- **Frequent**

  Children learn by getting plenty of feedback, so keep making the effort to praise or reward him every time, throughout the day.

- **Balanced**

  Just like the rest of us, children respond well to positive feedback. If they feel you are telling them off more often than you are praising them, they will soon get demotivated.

It could get worse before it gets better!

Some children are used to certain behaviours producing a result. For instance, they may have learned from experience that if they have a tantrum in the supermarket they will get some sweets to keep them quiet.

If you then refuse to buy the sweets when the child has a tantrum, at first his tantrums may get even worse as he tries harder and harder to produce the reward he expects – in other words, the behaviour can get worse before it gets better.

But hang on in there – behaviour that does not produce any rewards will eventually fade out. Provided you make sure there is no pay-off, the behaviour will fade away in time.

Sometimes problem behaviours do rear their ugly heads again after a little while, for no clear reason. But stand your ground and don't reward the behaviour – it will quickly fade away again.

Focus on the positive

We've all been there – there is something your child does that really bothers you and you have tried everything to get him to stop, but nothing seems to work. It seems as though you spend all your time nagging him or telling him off. Or you tell him to stop doing it and he does, but he does something else equally annoying. So it's time to try a different tack.

Rather than trying to stop a problem behaviour, the secret is to choose some other behaviour that you would like to take the place of the problem behaviour, and encourage that instead. This "target" behaviour should be one that is related to the problem behaviour but the child cannot do them both at the same time.

For instance, instead of telling your child 'Don't keep getting out of bed', you can frame it in a different way by saying 'I want you to stay in bed once you have gone to bed'. You can reward him when he achieves this.

Rather than telling your child *not* to do something, giving him a target behaviour to aim at can help you both to feel more positive. And it produces behaviour which you can then encourage by giving him rewards – so it becomes a win-win situation!

Here's some examples of target behaviour.

Problem behaviour	Target behaviour
Shouting	Talking quietly
Kicking the cat	Stroking the cat nicely
Drawing on the wallpaper or other inappropriate places	Colouring a picture

Choosing a target behaviour

Choose a target behaviour that is fairly easy for the child to achieve. The idea is that he experiences success and then you can reward and strengthen the behaviour. Praise him as soon as he shows the slightest sign of it!

If it is too big a challenge, break it down into smaller steps – if his bedroom is really messy, expecting him to clear it all up in one go might be too much to expect. So break down the task into manageable tasks, for instance, asking him to tidy up one area of the room at a time.

Providing triggers and pay-offs for the target behaviour

You might need to think of things to do both before and after the target behaviour that will support and maintain it. For example, if you want your child to go to bed on time, you might need to establish a calming before-bedtime routine to help him settle – a bath and a bedtime story, for example. If you want him to wash his face and clean his teeth in the morning, you could put up a picture or a sign in the bathroom to prompt him.

After the behaviour you will need to reward him, for instance with praise, attention, a treat or a star for his reward chart (see **page 37**).

CHOOSING A TARGET BEHAVIOUR

What behaviour would you like to stop? _____

_____

_____

Choose an alternative or target behaviour
that you would like to see instead _____

_____

_____

Think of some triggers that might
support the target behaviour _____

_____

_____

Think of some pay-offs you can give
to reward the target behaviour _____

_____

_____

HOW TO INCREASE "WANTED" BEHAVIOUR

What to do beforehand

- **Turn the problem behaviour on its head – encourage an alternative positive behaviour**
- **Tell your child what you expect him to do from now on**
- **Give calm, clear instructions**
- **Use your voice and body language to show you mean business**

Desired behaviour

What to do afterwards

- **Notice the behaviour**
- **Show your pleasure and give plenty of praise**
- **Give rewards and treats**
- **Use non-verbal rewards too – smile, wink, hug**

Reward charts

One way to use rewards is to draw up a reward chart. Each time your child does the specific behaviour you are trying to encourage, you can stick a star on the chart or colour in the appropriate space for that day.

A reward chart is a short-term way of encouraging certain behaviour and helps you to reward your child in a systematic way. It provides a structure for you to notice and reward positive behaviours.

Your child can see from the chart that he has earned a certain number of stars or stickers for doing a particular task or for learning a new skill.

Young children will be motivated by the chance of earning stickers alone, and for your praise and approval.

Older children will need other rewards, such as treats and being allowed to do certain things that they want to do. They can have these rewards when they have earned a certain number of stars or stickers.

Get him to decorate a special folder or container to keep his tokens in.

Look back at the list on **page 31** for some possible rewards that could work with your child. Here are some examples:

- A favourite snack
- A trip to the park
- Going swimming
- A cinema trip
- Having a friend to play
- Playing on the computer
- Spending some time with a special person, e.g. a favourite aunt
- A bedtime story
- Baking cakes
- Small gifts, e.g. magazine, hair clips
- Being allowed to stay up late one night

For a reward chart to work well, you need to think it through carefully first and make sure you take into account your child's needs, abilities and motivation.

Using tokens

Token systems can work well with four to seven-year-olds. With older children, you can use points rather than tokens, and keep a record of how many points the child has earned.

Token systems work in a similar way to star charts. They can be effective with children who need an immediate and concrete reward when they behave in the right way. When the child does what you have agreed he will do, you give him a token to reinforce the behaviour.

Just as with a reward chart, you identify a variety of rewards and decide how many tokens will be needed to earn each reward. The child can "cash in" the tokens or vouchers to earn rewards. The system can be as simple or sophisticated as you want to make it. For instance, older children might be able to cash in some tokens for small everyday rewards and save some for a bigger and longer-term reward such as a special trip.

It works best if they spend most of their tokens on short-term or medium-term rewards, such as things they will do that day or that weekend.

You might decide that your child can earn bonus tokens if he has done the task every day – for instance, if he has done some homework every night he can earn an extra token at the weekend.

The token could be, for instance, a button or even a special voucher which you have designed on the computer. Tokens are convenient and you can take them anywhere, so if your child is behaving well while you are out you can give him tokens to reward him.

The golden rules

- **Be specific** about the behaviour you want to see. 'Be good while we are out shopping' is too general. Instead you might say, 'I want you to stay by my side when we are in the supermarket'.

- **Go for small steps.** Children work better for small goals they can achieve more easily, and they need frequent rewards. So break the task down into more manageable bits and give him a sticker or token for each bit of the task. The more you can reward success, the more he will be motivated to behave better next time.

- **Follow it through.** The reward programme will work only if you notice the "desired" behaviour and reward it straight away.

- **Pace your steps.** Once your child is managing the task, you can make it more challenging – he then has to do a little more to achieve each sticker or token.

- **Keep rewards simple.** Don't make them too expensive or time-consuming.

- **Go for quick rewards.** Don't make the rewards take too long to earn – children will give up if rewards are too slow in coming.

- **Tackle just one or two behaviours at first.** If you try to tackle too many at a time, it will be difficult for both of you. Older children may be able to work on more tasks at a time.

- **Involve your child.** Talk to him about setting up the reward programme and deciding on the rewards. He may be able to help you draw or decorate the chart too. It will work better if he sees it as something he is doing with you rather than something you are imposing on him.

- **Be flexible.** Over time you may want to change the tasks or rewards.

- **Be positive.** If your child doesn't manage a task, be upbeat and say something like: 'You didn't get any stickers today, but I'm sure you will tomorrow.'

- **Let your child keep what he's earned.** Don't remove stickers, tokens or rewards as a punishment. Any discipline or punishment should be kept separate from the reward programme.

- **Make sure you're the one in charge of rewards.** Don't leave stickers, tokens or rewards around the house for your child to help himself to!

Over time, tangible rewards can be spaced out and eventually faded out altogether. But remember to keep on giving praise and encouragement to keep the good behaviour going.

Five steps to devising a reward programme

The behaviour I want to reward is:
(Be positive, clear and specific)

_____

1 **What exactly will my child need to do in order to get a sticker?** (Be specific!)

_____

_____

_____

2 **When and how will I check that my child is doing this?**

_____

_____

_____

_____

3 **I expect my child to earn around** _____ **stickers a day**

_____

_____

_____

4 **The rewards we have chosen and the number of stickers required for each reward are:**
(Make sure you discuss with your child what kind of rewards he wants to work for)

_____

_____

_____

5 **Make the chart – he can help to draw it or decorate it and go with you to buy the stickers**

_____

_____

_____

Here are two sample reward charts:

OVER TO YOU

Try using the reward chart or token system for a week. To help you see how it is working, fill in your results below

DAY OF PROGRAMME	STICKERS/TOKENS/ REWARDS EARNED	COMMENTS
1		
2		
3		
4		
5		
6		
7		

If it is going well...

Well done! If your child has made good progress and has been earning lots of rewards, you might decide that it's time to move things on – perhaps by expecting him to do a little more to earn each sticker or token, or by requiring more tokens to get a reward.

For instance, suppose your goal was to get your child to eat his breakfast more quickly. If he has managed to do it in 30 minutes this week you might want to make next week's target 20 minutes. Or perhaps you want to introduce a different target behaviour into the programme now.

Revising the programme keeps it interesting and challenging.

Discuss this with your child and tell him that he is doing so well that you think he is capable of achieving even more.

If it's not going well...

If your reward programme hasn't worked as well as you hoped, try to identify where the problem might lie. This checklist could help you see if you have all the right elements in place:

- Are you being clear and specific about the behaviour you wish to see?
- Is the behaviour too much for your child to manage? Could you break it down into smaller parts to make things a bit easier?
- Does your child understand that he is being rewarded, and what he is being rewarded for?
- Do you always notice the behaviour and reward it straight away?
- Is your child able to earn enough stickers to keep him motivated?
- Does it take him too long to earn a reward?
- Does he find the rewards fun and exciting? Or do you need to think more creatively about the rewards?
- Are you managing to apply the rewards consistently or do you sometimes forget or not have the time?
- Are you giving the rewards only when your child does what you want him to do, or do you sometimes weaken and give them anyway, even if he has not quite done the task?
- Do you give more praise and rewards than criticism in the course of a day?
- Are you giving plenty of praise and attention along with tangible rewards?
- Have you made it fun?

Changing your reward programme

Once you have looked at the results and asked yourself the questions above, write down in this box any changes that you decide to make to your reward programme.

Discuss this with your child. Would he like to change the tasks he is working on? How does he feel about the rewards?

What we will change	We will change it to	This is why we need to make the change
_____	_____	_____
_____	_____	_____
_____	_____	_____
_____	_____	_____
_____	_____	_____

Reward charts usually work best over a period of a few weeks and then they can be phased out. Naturally, you have to continue giving praise and encouragement, smiles, hugs and pats on the back!

Some goals will be achieved quickly, others will take time and patience.

Gold stars to tackle jealousy

Betty had a nine-year-old girl, Carina, placed with her. She already had another nine-year-old girl called Gemma in placement and it was clear that Carina was jealous of Gemma. Carina found it difficult when Betty gave Gemma any attention. She picked fights with Gemma and tried to bully her.

Betty set up a reward chart for Carina. If Carina did anything helpful or positive towards Gemma, she earned a gold star. When she got 10 stars, her reward was to go and stay overnight with Betty's sister, which was a special treat for her.

To avoid singling Carina out as the "difficult" child and to prevent Gemma from feeling left out, Betty also set up a reward chart for Gemma so that she could work on keeping her bedroom tidy.

'She responds so well to rewards'

Six-year-old Chantelle is hyperactive and has learning difficulties, and her behaviour presents quite a challenge for foster carer Stella.

'She can't sit down – she is always running around, diving on the sofa and throwing things,' says Stella. 'So I have a book that she calls her "Well done stickers book". She is very keen to earn points. If she can sit down for five minutes and listen to a story, she gets a sticker. When she gets upset, if she doesn't throw things around, she gets a sticker. She likes being in the kitchen, doing things, so her daily reward is to do some cooking. I give her cookery books and she chooses something she would like to cook, like fairy cakes, and we sit down and bake together.

'She doesn't like it when she gets less stickers than usual. At the end of the week, if she has earned five stickers on three days, she gets £5 in her piggy bank. She is saving up for a doll's buggy. She'll say: "I've done really well!"'

'They felt good about earning rewards'

'Charlie would run up and down the aisles when we went to the supermarket and it was a real problem,' says foster carer Sally. 'So I used a sticker chart with him and his sister. As a reward, the one who had most stickers at the end of the week got to choose what we did – going to the park, going bowling or having a school friend round, little treats that made them feel special. If we ran out of stickers, we would use buttons. Rosie would earn a button if, instead of getting tearful she came and told me how she felt. She would say to me, "I didn't cry, did I?" and I would say, "No, that deserves a button".

'At the end of the week I would make a big fuss of them and they felt good about earning these rewards. It certainly worked for these two.'

5 How to be good at giving instructions

KEEP INSTRUCTIONS SIMPLE

When you ask your child to put her dirty plate in the sink, go to bed or pick up her coat and hang it up, does she refuse, argue or simply ignore you? The way you ask a child to do something is important because it can make it either more or less likely that she will do as she is told.

This chapter will give you ideas on improving the way you communicate with your child when you are giving instructions.

Don't expect too much

Of course, no child does as she is told 100 per cent of the time – that would be an unrealistic expectation. Just like the rest of us, children have their own priorities and preferences and they don't want to do what someone else tells them all the time. Many looked after children come from families where there are no rules, or where adults apply rules inconsistently, and they have been able to do more or less what they want.

So carers need to set up new patterns of managing everyday interactions with the child, which will influence how co-operative she is likely to be.

How things can go wrong

A lot of conflict in families arises from everyday interactions that go wrong – simple requests or instructions that escalate into a full-blown argument or confrontation. Children can be very good at avoiding things they don't want to do. They may have learned that if they shout and complain enough, the adult will not follow through on his or her instructions and they can get away without doing whatever it is they were told to do. In these situations the child's inappropriate behaviour (ignoring, complaining or shouting) is rewarded because she avoids having to do what she was asked to do.

With a child like this, some carers become more and more reluctant to give instructions because they know the child is likely to make a scene or refuse to do as she is told. This might make life easier for the adult in the short term, but in the longer term it makes matters worse as it teaches the child that behaving badly pays off, and they also avoid learning about the skills and responsibilities that are part of growing up.

The other thing that often happens is that the adult gets frustrated and decides to make a stand. He or she starts to shout and make threats to try and force the child to give in. This rather threatening and aggressive behaviour might have the effect of making the child obey. But in the long term it doesn't help anyone. The adult feels that the only way to get the child to behave is to shout and threaten, and children pick up the message that you can get your way by being aggressive and threatening.

How NOT to give instructions

Researchers have identified six common mistakes many of us make when we are giving instructions to children. When we make these mistakes, children are *less* likely to do as they are told.

1   **Too many instructions.** Bombarding a child with instructions can overwhelm her and makes it less likely that she will comply.

2   **Chain instructions.** When you string a lot of instructions together – 'I want you to pick up your books from the floor, put the videos straight, put the chairs back where

they were and take your bag upstairs' – it makes it difficult for the child to remember everything. She is almost bound to forget one or two of the instructions, so will fail to do everything you asked.

3   **Vague instructions.** When you say things like 'Be careful' or 'That's enough', you know what you want but the child does not necessarily understand. Some of us feel uncomfortable telling a child what to do, so we make statements like 'Your coat is on the floor' when what we really mean is 'Please pick up your coat and hang it up now'.

4   **Framing instructions as questions.** Asking questions like 'Would you like to put your toys away now?' or 'Are you ready for your bath?' blurs the distinction between a question and an instruction. It provides the option for the child to say 'No', which is not what you want to hear!

5   **Giving an instruction followed by an explanation.** This makes your instruction less clear. It makes it easier for your child to get you into an argument about it, which will distract you from the issue. It's better to give your explanation first, followed by a clear instruction.

6   **"Let's…"** instructions. Don't say things like 'Let's get ready for bed' if you have no intention of getting into your own pyjamas! The child will feel you have misled her.

Remember your body language

It's not only what you say that counts, it's the way you say it. The child will be more likely to take you seriously if your non-verbal behaviour shows you mean business:

- Stand, rather than sit, when you give your child an instruction
- Get within arm's length of the child and make eye contact
- Use the child's name
- Speak firmly and clearly

How it's done

When giving instructions, do the following.

- Choose your time carefully. Most children hate to be interrupted when they are absorbed in a game or a programme. If you can, wait until a child has finished what she's doing or there is a break.
- Get close to the child and get her attention.
- Tell her what to do.
- Give her a few seconds to do what you've asked.
- If she co-operates, praise her.
- If she doesn't do what you have asked, repeat your instruction. Warn her that you will use a specified consequence if she doesn't co-operate (see Chapter **8** for more about consequences).
- If she co-operates, praise her. If not, use the back-up consequence.

• • • • • • • •

Giving clear and calm instructions: the key points

1 **Get her attention.** Get your child to listen to you by making eye contact, using her name and speaking slowly and clearly yet firmly.

2 **Be brief.** Long explanations will just encourage her to question you or argue.

3 **Be clear.** Make sure your child knows exactly what you want her to do: 'Move your cup further onto the table' is better than 'Be careful!'

4 **Be positive.** Tell her what to do rather than what not to do. 'Please speak quietly' is better than 'Stop shouting'.

5 **Give one instruction at a time.** Allow her to do what you asked and praise her before you tell her to do anything else.

6 **Be polite.** We often betray our annoyance or criticism by the tone of our voice or our choice of words ('How many times have I told you to…?'. Try to avoid putting the child down.

7 **Be realistic.** For instance, if a child has poor concentration and you tell her to spend 30 minutes alone doing her homework, she won't be able to manage it. Only ask her to do things she is capable of doing.

8 **Give warnings and reminders.** If a child is wrapped up in a game or programme, it can be helpful to give a warning that you are going to want her to do something soon: 'When this programme ends you must go to bed.' This provides time for the child to get used to the idea.

9 **Give options.** If you are going to stop a child doing something she enjoys, try to provide an alternative: 'You can't play with your ball in the house, but you can set the train set out instead if you like.'

10 **Avoid arguments.** Ignore the child's protests and arguments. Giving attention will just reward these. You can provide explanations at another time if you need to.

11 **Give "When…then…" instructions.** With older children, you may want to give them some choice over whether to comply or not. Offer an incentive for the child to do what you ask, while implying that she has a choice: 'When you have done your reading, then you can watch some television.'

12 **Follow through with praise or a consequence.** If the child co-operates, reward her. Praising her encourages her to co-operate next time. But if the child refuses to do what you ask, don't just ignore this – you must follow it through – otherwise she will learn to ignore your instructions. If she doesn't do as she is told, there must be some consequences.

Remember the ABC analysis of behaviour? Your instruction is like the antecedent or trigger. The way we give instructions has a big impact on the way the child responds.

'I learned not to shout'

Stella says: 'The Fostering Changes *course was very helpful in that before, I would have shouted more at Chantelle. Shouting just makes the child scared of the adult. Now, I take my time explaining. I give a warning and count to three. She will say "All right" and do it.*

'I can see real progress. Before, she wouldn't stop what she was doing to even look at you when you spoke to her. Now she will stop, look at you and listen and give you an answer.'

'I talk to her more calmly now'

Heather says that, before attending the Fostering Changes **course, she used to make mistakes with three-year-old Sarah. She feels that a lot of mothers do the same thing when they are tired or stressed and the kids are getting on their nerves.**

'Instead of telling them something quietly and calmly, you shout "Put that down! Don't do that! Come here!" and you don't realise you are giving them too much information and they can't take it all in. Going on the course helped me look at myself and be calmer when I'm talking to her.

'It's better to give an instruction and try not to push it all at once. For example, sometimes there are toys all over the place in Sarah's room. I used to shout to her from outside her room: "Pack away your toys, put your shoes away, pick those up, put that in the cupboard…"

'Now I go down to her level, I make sure we have eye contact and I say: "Sarah, pack away your toys". Sometimes it might take a bit of time but I would come to her, look at her and say it again. I found it very helpful. Obviously I couldn't change her overnight, but her response was good.'

6 Using "ignoring" to improve behaviour

Up to now in this programme, we have been looking at skills that encourage and reward a child. This chapter looks at a strategy that you can use to discipline a child. It works particularly well with behaviours where the child is playing up largely to get attention.

Here's how it works

Jamie is drawing with his carer. He starts throwing his pencils on the floor. His carer ignores this – she turns away, not speaking to him or looking at him any more. As soon as he carries on drawing or picks up a pencil, the carer turns back round to him and says: 'You've picked up a pencil. Good boy. And now you're drawing some beautiful green grass. I like that.'

For a child, attention is a very powerful motivator. Much of children's behaviour is strengthened when adults pay attention to it. Positive attention from an adult acts as a reward.

However, some children have such a deep need for adult attention that they will do whatever they can to get it, even if the attention comes in the form of criticism, shouting and telling off.

This can happen when children have learned that adults ignore them when they are quiet or behaving appropriately. In this situation, children quickly learn that the best way to get attention from adults is to play up and misbehave. This may be the experience your child had before he came to you.

Many of us do resort to shouting at children and telling them off when we are under pressure. But this means we are rewarding misbehaviour by giving it our attention, rather than correcting it. It is much better for the child to learn that if he behaves appropriately, he will get the attention he wants.

Use your attention as a "reward" for appropriate behaviour. Withdraw your attention – so that there is no pay-off – when the child's behaviour is inappropriate.

Ignoring misbehaviour is one of the ways you can influence the way he behaves.

For instance, if a child realises that making silly noises gets him no attention but talking in his normal voice means his carer will pay attention and listen to him, he will soon stop making silly noises.

Target positive behaviour

Simply ignoring the behaviour won't tell the child how he should behave – we also need to target the positive behaviour we want to see and provide rewards for that.

Who gets the attention?

Two children are eating their lunch. One is playing with her food and throwing it around. The other is getting on with eating. Many adults will automatically tell off the child who is messing with her food. But why not use your attention more strategically? Ignore the child who is messing about with her food and give praise and attention to the child who is getting on with eating.

What behaviour can you ignore?

There are lots of annoying but fairly harmless behaviours which you can safely ignore. For instance:

- Moaning
- Whining
- Silly noises and voices
- Nail-biting
- Pulling faces
- Complaining
- Minor squabbles
- Fiddling
- Tantrums
- Rudeness
- Swearing
- Messy eating
- Nose-picking

Which behaviour is not suitable?

Obviously, if the child is doing something dangerous to himself or others or being destructive, you will need to put a stop to it straight away – so ignoring it is out of the question. And there may be other things your child does that you personally find so stressful or difficult that you know you won't be able to manage to ignore them. Ignoring works best with minor irritating behaviours.

Ignoring should never be a way of expressing your own feelings

Some carers are struggling with feelings of frustration, anger and disappointment and can fall into the trap of very obviously "ignoring" the child as a way of showing how they feel. Take care to use ignoring only as a very specific and focused way of withdrawing your attention from certain behaviour, for as long as it lasts.

Isn't it cruel to ignore a child?

Ignoring should never be used as a punishment. You should use it selectively, to withdraw attention from minor irritating behaviour. Ignoring the child for long periods is unfair and unkind.

Only ignore one or two behaviours – target any more than this, and you will be spending too long ignoring the child and he will start to feel neglected.

What's so good about ignoring?

- The child gets no attention when he behaves badly, so bad behaviour goes unrewarded.

- It is a great alternative to nagging, shouting and so on – it can help you feel calmer.

- It keeps a positive relationship with the child.

- It makes you a good role-model for the child – you demonstrate the art of keeping your cool in the face of provocation!

Ignoring: how to do it

Ignoring involves not making eye contact, not speaking to or touching the child, and turning away from him.

- Decide which behaviours you are going to ignore (don't choose anything that stresses you out too much).

- Explain to the child what you are going to do.

- Be sure you are prepared to see things through.

OVER TO YOU

Choose one or two behaviours that you will ignore over the next week.
Make a note of the behaviours here.
Behaviour I will ignore:

1 _____

_____

_____

_____

2 _____

_____

_____

_____

Use the charts below to make a note of when you use the strategy and what effect it has. Make a mark in column 2 every time the behaviour occurs on that day.

Tip for carers: get on with tidying up, reading the newspaper, or talking with someone else when you are ignoring the child. You may need to keep yourself calm by making coping, positive statements.

BEHAVIOUR 1:

DAY	HOW MANY TIMES THE BEHAVIOUR OCCURS	TOTAL	EFFECT OF IGNORING
1			
2			
3			
4			
5			
6			
7			

BEHAVIOUR 2:

DAY	HOW MANY TIMES THE BEHAVIOUR OCCURS	TOTAL	EFFECT OF IGNORING
1			
2			
3			
4			
5			
6			
7			

BEHAVIOUR 3:

DAY	HOW MANY TIMES THE BEHAVIOUR OCCURS	TOTAL	EFFECT OF IGNORING
1			
2			
3			
4			
5			
6			
7			

BEHAVIOUR 4:

DAY	HOW MANY TIMES THE BEHAVIOUR OCCURS	TOTAL	EFFECT OF IGNORING
1			
2			
3			
4			
5			
6			
7			

BEHAVIOUR 5:

DAY	HOW MANY TIMES THE BEHAVIOUR OCCURS	TOTAL	EFFECT OF IGNORING
1			
2			
3			
4			
5			
6			
7			

Did you find ...

- ...the behaviour got worse before it got better? This is because at first the child may misbehave even more in an attempt to gain your attention. See it through! Sooner or later he will realise that it doesn't work – and that the way to get your attention is to behave well.

- ...the number of times the behaviour was occurring in a day had reduced by the end of the week? This is evidence of your success – ignoring a particular behaviour makes the child less likely to repeat it.

Still struggling?

- Try using more distraction. For instance, ignore the fact that the child is picking an argument with his sister and suggest that he helps you put out the bread and cakes for tea instead.

- Remember to combine ignoring with attending and lots of praise. Ignoring only works when the child experiences the contrast between ignoring and positive, warm attention.

- Make sure no-one else in the household is providing a pay-off for the behaviour that you are ignoring. Remove the child to a quiet place if you have to.

'I stopped reacting'

Six-year-old Peter and his eight-year-old brother David had suffered chronic and serious neglect. One of Peter's problem behaviours when he was placed with foster carer Colleen was that he would urinate around the house.

Colleen says: 'I was always having to think on my feet because he was always one step ahead of me – the Fostering Changes course gave me new ideas on how to manage things. I used ignoring a lot more. When he urinated, I stopped reacting – I would just say "OK" and calmly ask him to help clean it up. I didn't question him about why he had done it, which I would have done before. He looked quite taken aback – it surprised him.'

7 Setting limits

Many looked after children have lived with adults who have never set any boundaries for them or who have been inconsistent. This means they have missed out on the chance to develop a sense of inner stability and self-control.

As a carer, you can make up for this to some extent. You can provide care, warmth, sensitive responding and praise. You can also provide guidelines to provide safety and protection for the child, to contain her sometimes challenging behaviour and to help her learn how to get along with other people.

All children naturally want to do their own thing and don't always do as they are told – this can be seen as a healthy sign of independence. But when children hardly ever do as they are told, life can become frustrating and exhausting for their carers.

This chapter looks at setting limits and boundaries for children. Chapter 8 will look at what to do when children cross those boundaries and misbehave.

Discipline

We all have our own ideas about what "discipline" means and what we expect from a child. We all have our own disciplinary style – some believe in being firm but fair, others are warmer and less strict. And of course most of us are flexible and our styles vary depending on the situation and the needs of the child.

Looked after children: why discipline is different

When it comes to discipline, there are some issues that apply when working with looked after children that don't necessarily apply with your own children. For instance:

- You have to comply with your fostering agency's guidelines on control, restraint and discipline.

- Fostering legislation in England and Scotland makes it clear that smacking, slapping and other forms of corporal punishment are not acceptable.

- Social workers have their own personal and professional values and judgments which may not be the same as yours (or even the agency's). As a carer you can sometimes be given unclear or mixed messages, which makes it harder to know what to do in some situations.

- Some carers feel vulnerable to child protection allegations – they feel that if they take a firm line on discipline, it could be misconstrued and used against them.

- Carers are also only too aware that some looked after children have experienced physical and emotional abuse. They may fear that the child's previous experience will affect the way she feels when they have to discipline her.

Safe caring

In the context of foster caring, "safe caring" means relating to the child in a way that is:

- Safe and respectful for the child; and

- Safe for foster carers, in that they do not lay themselves open to misunderstandings or to allegations of abuse.

The strategies in this programme represent "safe caring". They involve treating the child with respect. They allow carers to plan their responses in advance, to respond in more rational and consistent ways and to avoid heated and impulsive reactions.

These are the principles of the programme, which are consistent with safe caring.

- The carer explains the strategies calmly in advance, at a neutral moment, so the child knows what will happen if she behaves in a certain way.

- The carer makes sure the child knows why she is going to use this approach.

- Discipline is most effective when it is used in a calm, rational and consistent way, not in a state of anger or heightened emotion.

- When a child's behaviour is particularly difficult or challenging, carers will need support – they may need to discuss with the agency the strategies they are using and the reasons for them.

- Carers have to be scrupulously fair about the child's rights – if they take anything from the child as a consequence for misbehaviour, such as money or a possession, they will need to put it in safe keeping.

- Carers need to take records of the child's behaviour and the strategies they are using, particularly in situations of conflict.

It is easier for children to behave well if they know what is expected of them. Looked after children who come to you may be used to very different standards of behaviour from those of your family. So drawing up some family rules is a good idea – it tells them how you expect them to behave.

Family rules

Everyone has their own priorities – good table manners might be a big issue for one carer but completely unimportant to another.

How to come up with your rules

- Think about the things that matter to you and the rest of the family, including the child herself.

- Get the whole family together to discuss and agree on the rules.

- Decide on five to ten rules.

- Make them clear and brief.

- If you can, make the rules say what everyone should, rather than should not, do: 'Keep your hands and feet to yourself' rather than 'Don't hit or kick people'.

- The rules should be about behaviour you can observe – for instance, you can't see what happens at school or at the football club.

How to make the rules work well

- Write the rules down and pin them up on the wall.

- Make it clear that the rules apply to everyone in the house.

If a child breaks a rule…

- Get the child's attention.

- Explain that she has broken a rule and why that is a problem.

- Get the child to explain what she should have done.

- Tell her to do it.

- Praise her when she does it correctly.

Suppose there is a rule that you eat food only in the kitchen. You find your child is eating a bowl of cereal in the living room. Here's what you do:

1   Get the child's attention.

2   Simply and calmly tell her what the problem is: 'You have taken your cereal into the living room.'

3   Say briefly why that is a problem: 'You could spill it on the sofa or the carpet.'

4   Ask the child to tell you the appropriate behaviour: 'We are meant to eat in the kitchen.'

5   Ask her to do it.

6   Praise her for the right behaviour: 'Thank you for taking your cereal back to the kitchen to eat.'

Here's an example of one family's rules.

The rules at 10 Markham Place

We always try to tell the truth and be polite.

We always ask permission before taking things that belong to other people.

After eating, we take our plates out to the kitchen.

We speak kindly to the animals and always treat them gently.

We change out of our uniforms and put play clothes on when we come home from school.

We wash every day and clean our teeth after breakfast and after dinner.

We flush the toilet after we use it.

OVER TO YOU

My ideas
for some
family rules

Before you have a family discussion, start thinking about what you would like to include in the rules for your own family. Make some notes here.

_____

_____

_____

_____

_____

_____

_____

_____

_____

_____

_____

_____

_____

_____

- **Have a family discussion. Have a large sheet of paper in front of you so you can jot down everyone's thoughts and ideas.**

- **When you have all agreed on what the rules will be, write them down on the next page.**

- **You could get the child to design and produce a poster showing the rules, which you can stick up on the wall at home.**

- **See the family rules as "work in progress". After you have lived with the rules for a while you may decide you need to fine-tune or change them!**

Our family rules

_____

_____

_____

_____

_____

_____

_____

_____

_____

_____

_____

_____

_____

_____

_____

_____

_____

_____

_____

_____

Telling the child how her behaviour makes you feel

Don't overdo the use of "I..." messages. Use them too often and they will lose their impact and overburden the child with too much information about your feelings.

Sometimes children can behave in ways that leave us feeling angry, frustrated, upset, rejected or taken for granted. When we feel like this, the danger is that we give vent to our feelings by giving negative attention to the child in the form of telling her off, nagging her or losing our temper.

Discipline is most effective when we can do it calmly, without letting our negative feelings enter into it.

It's important for carers to have their own support networks – perhaps their partner or a sympathetic friend or group – so they can offload feelings like this. Talking about feelings with someone else means you are less likely to blow your top with the child.

But there are some times when it can be helpful to let the child know that you have needs and feelings too. There is a way to do this, calmly and assertively, without hurting or verbally attacking the child. And that is by giving an "I..." message. An "I..." message lets you take responsibility for your own feelings. It tells her how you feel, but without accusing or blaming her.

The usual way to do this is to say: 'When you (behave in a certain way), I feel…. because…'

For instance:

Message that lays blame on the child	"I..." message
'Your language is appalling and you never show me any respect.'	'When you swear at me, I feel really hurt because it seems as though you have no respect for me.'
'You treat this place like a hotel and I'm not your servant!'	'When you come in and drop your coat on the floor, I feel as though you are taking me for granted because I have to clear up after you.'

OVER TO YOU

Think about some of the times when you have told off the child (or someone else – this works with partners too!).

See if you can say the same thing, this time using an "I…" message instead. An "I…" message tells the child how her behaviour makes you feel. If it helps, write it down here.

What I said

What I could have said
('When you … I feel … because …')

_____   _____

_____   _____

_____   _____

_____   _____

_____   _____

_____   _____

_____   _____

_____   _____

_____   _____

_____   _____

_____   _____

_____   _____

8 Helping children learn from the consequences of their actions

This and the following chapter will give you two different strategies you can use when you need to discipline the child. They are a positive alternative to shouting and making threats, which some carers sometimes resort to when they are feeling low, tired and stressed. Shouting and threats tend to make most situations worse.

These positive strategies are:

● Natural and logical consequences (for minor repeated misbehaviour)
● Time-out from positive reinforcement – sometimes just called time-out for short (for more serious misbehaviour).

But you have to work on your relationship first...

These strategies can only work in the context of a positive relationship, where you have already established some kind of trust and bond with the child. So the first step is to create as positive, warm and rewarding a relationship with the child as you can. The strategies outlined in Chapters 2 and 3 (on praise and positive attention) will help you do this.

Learning from the results of our actions

We all learn about the world by observing the results of things we do – in other words, the consequences of our actions.

As children grow up, carers need to allow them to experience the consequences of their actions so that they learn about the world and develop their own sense of personal responsibility and competence.

However, we also need to nurture and protect them. We don't want them to learn from experience of the dangers of boiling water, electrical appliances and road traffic. With young children, we have to intervene when the consequence would be dangerous.

Natural consequences

Some consequences can be described as natural consequences – in other words, they are what happens when adults or others do not intervene to protect children from the results of their actions. As long as there is no danger involved, we may feel it is helpful and informative for the child to learn from certain actions:

- If he walks in puddles without wellies, he will get wet feet.
- If he doesn't eat his lunch, he will feel hungry by dinnertime.

Logical consequences

"Logical consequences" are consequences designed by carers and other adults as suitable consequences for certain behaviours. For instance:

- If the child plays football in the house, the carer will take his ball away.
- If he deliberately breaks his sister's toy, he will have to replace it out of his own pocket money.
- If he refuses to wipe his feet and brings mud into the house, he will have to clear it up.
- If he is late for school, he gets a detention.

The child is held accountable for his behaviour and experiences a consequence that is mildly unpleasant as a result.

Using logical consequences with children

Looked after children with challenging behaviour, like any other children, need to learn about the consequences of their behaviour. If there are no negative consequences when they misbehave, they may well carry on behaving in ways that are inappropriate, anti-social and self-destructive.

Most of us prefer to avoid conflict if we can. And disciplining children does involve conflict. But as adults and carers we do need to help children learn that if they misbehave, there will be consequences. Letting children "get away with it" does not do them any favours in the long term.

You can use simple logical consequences even with children as young as two. You can use an 'If…then…' sentence to explain it to them: 'If you throw your food around, then I will take it away.'

Doing this:

Carers can come up with logical consequences which they can apply as a response to a child's undesirable behaviour.

- Holds the child accountable for what he does
- Helps him make the link between his behaviour and the consequences.

Guidelines for natural and logical consequences

● Discuss the consequences in advance

Warn the child of the consequences of his behaviour beforehand. He needs to know that if he does not do his homework, he will not be allowed to play on the computer, rather than having this sprung on him: 'You haven't done your homework, so you can't play on the computer.'

When children know about the consequences in advance, they have a chance to decide how they want to respond. This helps them learn to take responsibility for their decisions – and teaches them that, in many situations, it is to their advantage to behave well.

● Consequences should be appropriate

In some situations we can allow children to learn from natural consequences – but clearly, we would not allow them to fiddle with electrical sockets and appliances to learn about the properties of electricity.

It would also be inappropriate to say: 'Because you bit your sister I am going to bite you.' This would model inappropriate behaviour, would cause pain and would be hurtful.

Don't threaten the child with consequences that are way too severe – like cancelling their birthday party or making them miss a family trip to Disneyland. You will find that you either can't follow it through or, if you do, you will alienate and hurt the child. If you can't think of an appropriate consequence on the spot, you can tell the child that you need time to decide what the consequence will be.

● **Consequences should be immediate**

Children can't relate to consequences that are too far ahead, such as cancelling a treat the following week. They are more likely to get the message if the consequences follow quickly and they have to do something straight away or at least within 24 hours. It's best to keep consequences short and to the point, so the child can quickly get on with positive activities again. If you take the child's playdough away for five minutes because he is throwing it around, make sure he gets the chance to play with it again so that you can praise him for playing with it properly this time.

You might decide to let the child learn from certain natural consequences. For instance, if he refuses to get out of bed, he will miss the school bus. If he refuses to take his coat to school, he will get cold or wet.

● **Consequences should be straightforward**

It's best to deliver any consequences in a calm and matter-of-fact way. Try to avoid lecturing the child, getting into arguments or listening to his protests and pleas. (Remember how attention from you will reward inappropriate behaviour.)

Avoid being too apologetic about it ('I'm really sorry you are going to have to miss your favourite programme now') or too critical ('Well, it serves you right!'). If you let your own feelings show, they will get in the way of the child's learning and the strategy will be less effective. The idea of this strategy is that the child learns from experiencing the negative consequences of his choices, not from your displeasure.

Do you struggle with the idea of setting consequences?

Setting logical consequences can be quite challenging if you are the kind of carer who instinctively draws back from situations of conflict. It might help if you remind yourself of the following:

● Children need boundaries, limits and consequences even if they protest and react against them.

● Making a child face consequences when he behaves badly will help him in the long term because he will learn to behave better and there will be less conflict in his life in the future.

● It is in the child's best interests for you to be firm and consistent in applying consequences.

● Progress with some children may be slow and painful, but it is still a move in the right direction.

Coming up with consequences

Think of some suitable logical consequences for the following behaviours and write them in the box.

Behaviour

Your child is playing dangerously on the seesaw at the playground

A possible logical consequence

_____

_____

Behaviour

Your child is playing roughly with a toy

A possible logical consequence

_____

_____

Behaviour

Your child is wandering away from you on a walk

A possible logical consequence

_____

_____

See below for some possible logical consequences.

Behaviour	A possible logical consequence
Your child is playing dangerously on the seesaw at the playground.	**He has to get off and sit on a bench for five minutes.**
Your child is playing roughly with a toy.	**You take the toy away for a short time (timing varies according to the age of the child – but it should be brief so that the child can have another go at playing more appropriately).**
Your child is wandering away from you on a walk.	**Your child has to walk with you, holding your hand, for the next few minutes.**

Using logical consequences

Here's an example of how it works:

- **Give a warning**: 'You must draw on the paper, not on the table. If you draw on the table I will put your crayons away for five minutes.'

- **If the child doesn't follow your instruction, withdraw the activity. Do it quickly. Don't get drawn into arguments.** 'You are drawing on the table and not on the paper, so I am putting the crayons away for five minutes.'

- **After the time has elapsed, return the activity to the child. This gives him the opportunity to play with the crayons again and do it properly this time. Make sure you praise him for drawing on the paper!**

- **If he carries on drawing on the table, take the activity away for longer.**

'No ice lolly for Sarah'	**Heather was fostering three-year-old Sarah and two younger boys. She would sometimes struggle to find the best way to manage Sarah's attention-seeking behaviour.**

'When I picked up the children from nursery, I would have three of them in the back of the car. Sarah would be kicking the seat or teasing the little ones, and when you're driving you can't really do anything, so I used to keep shouting at her and threatening her, saying: "You wait, when you get home you won't get that ice lolly".'

So the trips home from nursery were stressful for Heather. But after learning about logical consequences, she found a better way.

'When I collected them from nursery, I said to Sarah: "Listen, I am only going to tell you this once. While we are in the car, if you misbehave I am not going to shout at you but when we get home you will not have any sweets or ice cream".'

'She did misbehave, so when we got home I gave the boys an ice lolly but Sarah did not get one.

'She must have understood because the next time, she didn't do it again.'

OVER TO YOU

Consequences

Now think of one or two minor behaviour problems your child has that you would like to tackle. Think of a logical consequence you could apply to each of them.

Behaviour	A possible logical consequence
1 _____	_____
_____	_____
_____	_____
_____	_____
2 _____	_____
_____	_____
_____	_____
_____	_____

Over the next week, have a go at applying these consequences whenever necessary. Make a note of what happens, below.

DAY	BEHAVIOUR	CONSEQUENCE	COMMENTS/ OBSERVATIONS
1			
2			
3			
4			
5			
6			
7			

Did you notice a reduction in either of the behaviours over the course of the week? Keeping good records helps us to track changes accurately – to stick with strategies that are working and change approaches that are not effective.

If you did, the consequences are proving effective.

When things are not going well, remind yourself of times when you have set limits or applied consequences and the results have been positive.

If the problem behaviour has not reduced by the time you have applied the consequence several times, have another think about what you've been doing.

- Have you remembered to issue a warning first, so that the child has the chance to choose to stop misbehaving?

- Have you been applying the consequence immediately after the child misbehaves? Too long a gap and he won't make the connection.

- Are your logical consequences short and to the point? A consequence which is unrelated to the misbehaviour is confusing and if it takes too long it gets in the way of appropriate behaviour. Make sure the child gets back to positive activity straight after the consequence, so you can praise him for behaving well.

- Have you applied the consequence on every occasion the child has done this particular thing? If you are inconsistent, it will take him longer to learn.

- Have you been able to stay calm when you apply the consequence or have you been letting your own feelings of anger or anxiety show?

- Have you managed to avoid getting drawn into arguments with the child about the consequence? When you get into discussions with the child you are paying him extra attention – without knowing it, you could be rewarding the very behaviour that you are trying to get rid of.

9 Using "time-out"

SHE USED TO HAVE 'TIME OUT' IN HER BEDROOM BUT WE FIND MAKING HER WATCH RERUNS OF THE 'ANTIQUES ROADSHOW' IS **FAR** MORE EFFECTIVE!

©FRAN

Many looked after children have come from disrupted, chaotic, neglectful and even harmful backgrounds. They may have never experienced family life that is stable, predictable, warm and encouraging.

In Chapters 2 to 4 we explored different ways you can build up positive experiences for children and reward them for appropriate behaviour. Once children have learned that life can be more predictable and pleasant, they will not want to lose your positive attention.

"Time-out from positive reinforcement" – sometimes just called "time-out" for short – means withdrawing your attention in response to misbehaviour. It is a strategy you can use with fairly serious behaviour problems.

It means time-out from your positive attention. In other words, for a set period of a few minutes the child has to go to a particular place and while she is there you avoid talking to her or interacting with her in any way. Time-out must be used with sensitivity and care.

Using time-out

You may have heard the term "time-out" before – perhaps you even use a version of it yourself or you may know other carers who do. But people use this term to cover a variety of different disciplinary measures. Some people use what they call "time-out" in a harsh and abusive way, sending a child up to her room and completely ignoring her for long periods, regardless of how she is behaving. To use time-out properly, you need to understand the social learning principles behind it.

This chapter will show you how to use time-out appropriately, as a tool for managing difficult behaviour calmly and consistently while still respecting the child.

Time-out is something carers can use instead of more negative responses like arguing, shouting, blaming and criticising. It provides time and space for both you and the child to calm down. It's not an alternative to reasoning and discussion but it can be used when conflict is mounting and talking reasonably is no longer an option for either you or the child.

What behaviour will result in time-out?

Decide on one or two behaviours which will result in time-out, for example:

- She persistently refuses to do as she is told.
- She is being destructive.
- She is being aggressive.

Only apply time-out to one or two behaviours – if you use it for too many types of misbehaviour, you may end up over-using time-out and the child will not receive enough positive attention.

Where will time-out be?

For time-out, the child should be somewhere dull, away from television and activities so there is nothing to reward and interest her. Ideally, it should be somewhere you can see her. For young children, you can put a chair by a wall or in the hallway. It should be somewhere safe, so that the child cannot cause damage to herself or property during time-out. Bedrooms are not a good idea as they are often too interesting and you don't want to create an association between the bedroom and being disciplined for bad behaviour.

Don't put the child in a secluded place or shut or lock her in a room – you simply want to remove positive attention, not frighten or distress her. Looked after children may be more prone to experience isolation as frightening and rejecting – some may have had abusive experiences of enforced isolation and confinement.

How long should time-out be?

It should be brief – perhaps three minutes. However, the child should not be allowed out of time-out until she is quiet. She must be quiet in order to come out of it, even if she screamed and protested through most of it.

You will have to decide how long she has to be quiet for before she can come out of time-out. For some children it might be two minutes – for others, half a minute.

The first time you use time-out, the child may protest and scream and shout – which means time-out may go on for 20 or 30 minutes or even longer. But children learn very quickly that the sooner they quieten down, the sooner they can come out.

Explain it to the child beforehand

The child needs to know about time-out before you use it. This needs to be done when the child is calm – not just as they are being reprimanded for breaking a rule. Explain clearly which behaviours will result in time-out and what will happen.

For example: 'Sometimes you do naughty things that upset or hurt others. We are going to practice a way to help you stop this. When you pinch or bite your brother, you will go immediately to time-out. This means I will take you to the bottom step in the hall and you will have to sit there on your own for three minutes. I will not talk to you or give you any attention while you are there. When you have been quiet for the last minute, you will then be able to come out of time-out.'

Check that she has understood by getting her to tell you what will happen.

What to do when your child misbehaves

Make sure other members of the family understand time-out and do not reward the child by paying her any attention when she is in time-out.

Explain to the child what she has done and that she has to go to time-out. When she is there, do not interact with her in any way. Ignore crying, protests and minor misbehaviour. Get on with the washing up, reading the newspaper or housework or talk to someone else.

Coping with the child's reaction

Some children are fine with time-out. Others, of course, complain, threaten, cry or use other tactics to try and get out of the situation. They may say they feel unwell, or hungry, or say things that are calculated to make you feel bad or guilty.

This can be really upsetting and you may be tempted to give in. But you mustn't – the child needs to learn that she cannot get her own way by doing or saying things like this.

These early time-out experiences can be difficult for carers to cope with. Here are some ways you can help yourself to stay strong.

- Have your partner or a friend there to support you and help distract you so that you don't give in to the child's protests.

- Be confident that, used properly, time-out will not harm the child – in the long run, this experience will benefit her because it will help her learn to behave better. It is better for both of you if you can use time-out instead of losing your temper.

- To stay calm, take deep breaths and count to 10 or repeat a positive affirmation like: 'She is going to be OK. I will remain calm and firm for her.'

- Remind yourself that the first few times will be hard – but once the child learns that you do not give in, she will calm down much more quickly when she is in time-out. She will learn that she can get out of it sooner by being co-operative.

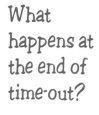

What happens at the end of time-out?

At the end of time-out, this is what you do.

- After time-out, do not tell the child off or even talk about what has happened.

- Do not insist that she apologises or shows remorse. She can learn her lesson without this.

- If the child had refused to carry out an instruction, repeat the instruction until she has done what you wanted.

- Encourage the child to get involved in some positive activity.

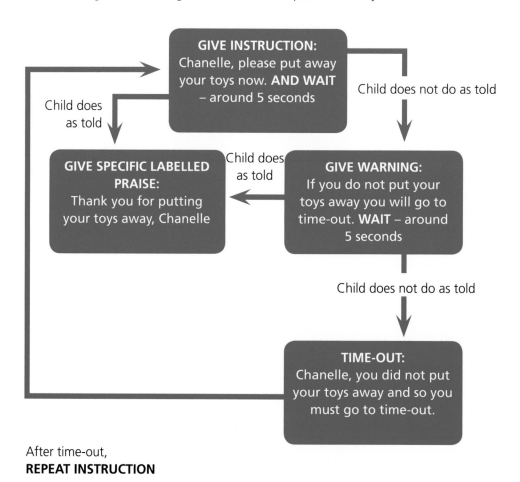

After time-out,
REPEAT INSTRUCTION

- As soon as you can, praise the child for something or look for a chance to "attend" (see Chapter 3). This shows her that you do not bear a grudge and the conflict is over.

When the child does not co-operate

- **If she refuses to go to time-out**

  With a young child, you can lead her firmly to the time-out place or chair. With an older child, avoid physical contact as it may come across as aggression. Instead, add time on to the time-out period. Add one or two minutes a time, up to a total of eight minutes' time-out: *As you have not done as I told you and gone into time-out, you will now have to stay in time-out for six minutes.*

  If she still won't co-operate, going over eight minutes will be unproductive. In this case, warn her that you will withdraw a privilege: *If you don't go into time-out now, you won't be able to watch television for the rest of the evening.*

- **If she comes out of time-out before she is allowed to**

  With a young child, return her to the place. If you have to stay with her to make sure she doesn't leave it, avoid talking or making eye contact. With an older child, use the strategy above – add on up to eight minutes and then withdraw a privilege.

- **If she is destructive in time-out**

  Do not let her get out of time-out by being destructive. With a child who is likely to be destructive, choose a place for time-out where there is nothing valuable that she could damage. Hold her accountable for what she does – afterwards, she must clear up any mess she has made or, if she has broken something, pay for a replacement out of her own money or lose a privilege.

- **If she refuses to come out of time-out**

  The child may try to turn it into a power struggle. You can choose to either ignore it or put her back in time-out so you remain in charge: *As you won't come out of time-out, you must stay there for four more minutes.*

Using time-out when you are out of the house

When you become more confident with time-out, you can use it out of the house too. At a wedding, party, restaurant or on a shopping trip, make it clear how you want the child to behave. Provide incentives for good behaviour and spell out the consequences of misbehaviour. If you need to use time-out, this could be in the car, on the stairs or somewhere else away from where she wants to be. (You might need to explain what you are doing to any concerned passers-by.)

"Calm-down time" with the under-fives

With young children, it is often enough to remove them from the activity and get them to sit quietly on the edge of the activity for a minute or two. Withdraw your attention. When they have calmed down, allow them to return to the activity. *You are throwing sand around in the sandpit, so you will have to come and sit on the side for two minutes. After that, you can go back to the sandpit to play.*

"CALM-DOWN TIME" FOR YOU

- When you are getting frustrated and annoyed with a child but you recognise that the problem is with you and not her, give *yourself* some "time-out" by removing yourself from the situation.

- Go off into another room for a cup of tea and listen to some music or have a walk round the garden. Or talk to your partner, a friend or your link worker from the fostering agency. Do whatever helps you calm down and avoid conflict.

OVER TO YOU

Think of one or two ways your child misbehaves that might be suitable for time-out:

When I could use time-out

1 _____

2 _____

3 _____

Which place will you use for time-out?

_____

_____

_____

How many minutes will time-out last?

_____

_____

_____

How long must your child be quiet for, before being allowed out of time-out?

_____

_____

_____

Explain time-out to your child.

Over the next few days, use the table on the next page to reflect on your experiences with time-out and track progress.

My experiences with time-out

DATE AND TIME	BEHAVIOUR	WHAT HAPPENED DURING TIME-OUT	WHAT HAPPENED AFTERWARDS

You should notice:

- The child calms down sooner each time.

- The targeted misbehaviour starts to become less frequent and/or less intense when you have used time-out on several occasions.

- You feel more and more confident about using time-out.

'Using time-out has helped me'

Time-out is one of the strategies Stella learned on the Fostering Changes course.

'When I started using time-out with Chantelle, being in her room made her angry and she would throw her toys and slam the door and cried and cried for so long. Because of how she is, time-out could go on and on and we didn't want her to spend so much time on her own in her room. So now time-out happens in our sitting room and when I say "time-out", I leave the room myself and go upstairs, leaving her on her own. It is very effective. It doesn't go on as long, because she wants me down there with her.'

---

10 Thoughts and feelings

I THINK THEY WANTED JUST THREE PROBLEM AREAS

What we tell ourselves about a situation affects how we feel about it, and therefore how we behave. This chapter will look at how we can transform negative and self-defeating patterns of thought into something that helps and empowers us to deal with situations.

Caring for children can be rewarding. But at times it also inevitably evokes uncomfortable emotions of anger, sadness, frustration and anxiety, and these emotions can sometimes affect the way we respond to children. But we can learn to explore these links and manage our own feelings more effectively.

Negative self-talk

According to cognitive theory, the way we think about an event determines our emotional response. It is the way we interpret the event – the meaning we give to it – that determines how relaxed or stressed we feel about it.

The term sometimes used to refer to negative and unhelpful thoughts is "negative self-talk".

Suppose a child helps himself to food out of the fridge and eats it in the living room, making a mess on the carpet. Here are two ways the carer might respond:

1   The carer might feel angry and hostile to the child.

    She might think: 'He is so selfish and inconsiderate! I cannot trust him for a moment!'

    In this state of mind, she is likely to criticise or shout at the child.

2   The carer might feel hopeless and demoralised.

    She might think: 'He takes no notice of what I say. Everyone walks over me. I have no authority.'

    In this state of mind, she is likely to complain to the child but not to be assertive or follow through with any consequences.

A more constructive take on the situation would be for the carer to think about it in a way that does not bring her down:

'He knows he shouldn't take food without asking and eat it in the living room. I need to go through the house rules with him again. In the meantime, he must come and clear up after himself.'

This is a more effective and assertive coping response and leaves the carer feeling more energised and motivated to tackle the problem.

So we sometimes make a difficult situation even worse for ourselves by the way we interpret and judge it. Our thoughts affect our reaction to it.

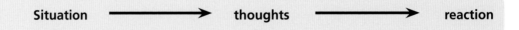

Situation ⟶ **thoughts** ⟶ **reaction**

Exploring difficult feelings

Think about the following points and write down what comes to mind:

● **How do you know when you are stressed? How does your body feel? What are the physical sensations?**

_____

_____

_____

_____

● **How does stress affect the way you behave?**

_____

_____

_____

_____

● **Think of three situations that make you feel stressed**

_____

_____

_____

_____

● **Now try to tease out the negative thoughts that you tend to have in those situations. What messages do you tend to give yourself? These messages are the negative self-talk that helps trigger the sensations of stress.**

_____

_____

_____

_____

The kind of messages that make us feel bad are often things like this:

I can't cope
He's out of control
I can't manage him
Nothing I do will work with him
It's hopeless
I'm useless
My life is a mess

In other words, we tend to beat ourselves up when things aren't going well. But when we do this, we are not helping ourselves!

Recognising negative thoughts

Our behaviour and feelings are both powerfully influenced by our thoughts. We recognise our feelings because we know the signs that we are stressed, sad, anxious and so on. We also know how we tend to behave when we are aware of these emotions.

In contrast, we are often less aware of our negative thoughts. Yet a negative thought can set in motion a chain of responses, so we need to recognise these thoughts.

When we have identified the negative thought or belief, we can then decide whether it is valid and replace it with a more constructive and coping thought. This takes practice.

In a nutshell, here's how it's done.

1   Notice unpleasant feelings, emotional responses and/or tension in the body – for instance, feeling anxious, jittery, churning stomach, sleeplessness.

2   Identify what was going through your head to make you feel this way.

3   Decrease the negative thoughts using a number of different strategies – which are outlined on pages **91** and **92**.

Signs of negative thinking

To identify negative thoughts, we need to know what to look for. These are some of the signs:

● **Generalisations**: 'He's selfish', 'She's greedy' – labels like these tend to imply that the problem is permanent and nothing will change it.

● **Exaggeration**: often involving words like "everybody", "nobody", "always" and "never" – 'I never get anything right', 'nobody ever listens to me'.

● **Extreme expectations**: No one is perfect yet some of us think we should be. For example, you might expect yourself never to lose patience with a child or always to have a clean and tidy house, and you feel like a failure when you can't live up to your own high expectations.

● **The "shoulds" and "oughts"**: We often have ideas about how things "ought" to be and how people "should" behave, but reality falls short of our ideals. This can leave us feeling let down, cheated and angry.

● **Mind-reading**: We may find ourselves making assumptions about other people's thoughts and feelings. 'I can't say no to him because he will blow his top'; 'she didn't phone me because she doesn't care about me.' These beliefs affect what we do and how we react – but the trouble is that our beliefs may be quite wrong.

● **Turning things into a catastrophe**: This is what we do when we think: 'That's the last straw' or 'I can't cope with another thing going wrong.' By telling yourself the situation is disastrous, you are making yourself feel desperate and powerless.

Negative thoughts make us feel more emotional – which impairs our ability to think and act rationally.

Decreasing negative thoughts

What we need to do is examine, challenge and reject our inaccurate negative thoughts. Then we need to replace them with thoughts that are more positive, constructive and helpful to us. Here are some examples:

● **Replace generalisations** with thoughts that are more specific and acknowledge the positives as well as the negatives. See below for some examples and see if you can add an example of your own:

> Generalisation
> **He's completely selfish and irresponsible.**
>
> More accurate thought
> **He can be self-absorbed, but at other times he is very thoughtful and kind.**
>
> Generalisation
> **I'm an insensitive person.**
>
> More accurate thought
> **Sometimes I make insensitive comments but most of the time I am understanding and caring.**
>
> Generalisation
> **Nobody ever listens to me.**
>
> More accurate thought
> **The children have not been co-operative today. But yesterday they were good and I will be more assertive with them tomorrow.**

● **Keep things in perspective**. In most situations you can remind yourself that, in your shoes, many other people would be feeling the same as you. Here are some examples – see if you can add another example of your own.

Seeing problems as extreme	Seeing problems as normal
When she screams at me I just can't stand it – I feel as though I'm going mad.	I feel all wound up and upset when she screams at me, but that's natural.
Today was the worst day ever and if things don't improve, I can't go on.	Everyone has bad days sometimes.
No other child would talk to me like that.	She is sometimes defiant, like lots of other looked after children.

● **Substitute more positive and coping thoughts.** When your thoughts are negative and bringing you down, try repeating something more calming and positive that will help you cope. Here are a couple of examples. Can you think of another?

Negative thought	Positive thought
Things can't get any worse.	This is difficult but it's not the end of the world. I can deal with it.
This child is totally disorganised and can't concentrate – she'll never do well at school.	She needs my support and encouragement to help her learn to focus and concentrate.

● **Dispute absolutes.** Stop striving for perfection, because you'll never reach it. Be more flexible and relaxed. For example:

Rigid expectations	Flexible expectations
I should cook a hot meal for the family every evening.	Who says it's always my job to cook? I'll let someone else take a turn – or make it easy on myself by getting a ready meal sometimes.
Ayesha should do as she is told, every time.	What makes me think she must be 100 per cent obedient? No child could manage that.

● **Don't try to mind-read.** If you assume you know about other people's intentions, you could get it wrong and get angry or upset for nothing. Instead, focus on the behaviour you want to change. This will leave you feeling more positive and in control. For example:

Mind-reading	Focus on behaviour
Jasmin has deliberately left her clothes on the floor because she knows it winds pick me up.	Jasmin has a problem with putting her clothes away. I'll talk to her about setting up a reward chart to encourage her to them up and put them away.
Robert chews with his mouth open because he knows we all hate it.	Robert needs to develop better table manners – how can we help him?

● **Be objective about situations.** Some people are prone to self-criticism and tend to blame themselves or take it personally when things go wrong. But this just makes you feel depressed and ineffectual. It's more constructive if you can step back and look at things less personally. For example:

Blaming yourself	Being objective
I'm a soft touch – I'm useless at getting Lauren to do anything for herself.	What would I like Lauren to do? How can I help her with this? What can I do differently?
Robbie accidentally broke our train set and now everyone is upset – it's my fault, I shouldn't have let him play with it.	I decided to give him the chance to play with it but it didn't work out the way I planned. Still, I can't watch him every minute. The children will have to accept that toys do sometimes break. We can replace the broken train.

● **Acknowledge your own strengths and abilities.** Most of us have a tendency to criticise ourselves far more than we praise ourselves! We need to learn to value our efforts and achievements and give ourselves a pat on the back sometimes. If you get into the habit of being kinder to yourself, your confidence and self-esteem will grow.

You can be a good role model for the child if you show him that it's OK to be positive about yourself and your achievements. Here are some examples. Can you think of any others?

You can say nothing...	Or you can model self-praise and positive thinking
	'I didn't overreact when our neighbour came to complain about your behaviour. I listened to him and was assertive and took action. I'm very pleased with myself.'
	'I think I organised your birthday party very well – everyone enjoyed the games and I was proud of the birthday cake I made for you.'

- **Use humour.** Laughter dispels any tension and helps us deal with situations more calmly. So try to avoid the tendency to take things too seriously. For example:

Taking things too seriously	Using humour
Your bedroom is a tip and it's a disgrace to the family. You have got to clear it up or it's going to become a serious health hazard.'	'Look at your room – for a minute, I thought we'd had burglars! Better take your dirty plates downstairs to the kitchen – or you might find little mice deciding to move in!'
'You haven't brushed your hair today. It's a mess. Go back to your bedroom and brush it. I don't want to be seen out with you like that.'	'Here's your hairbrush. Why don't you make yourself look beautiful before we go out?'
'The kids have all been squabbling and screaming all day. I can't stand this! It's just impossible!'	'The kids have been horrible today. They've excelled themselves. I think it's a plot to drive me mad. But they'll never win!'

Use coping statements

We have seen how you can challenge your own negative thoughts and replace them with more constructive thoughts.

Something else you can do is to use affirmations or "coping statements" to give yourself encouragement when things are tough. This is a form of "positive self-talk" which can help to keep you calm and give you courage to face difficult situations.

Coping statements should be short, start with "I..." and be in the present tense. Here are some examples:

Coping statements

I can get through this. I will cope.
I'm a good carer. He needs me to keep calm and remain firm.
I've done this before and I know it's going to be OK.
I need to just breathe slowly and stay calm.
I can do it. It will work.

OVER TO YOU

Think about some stressful situations you could have to face. Think about the kind of statements that would help to counteract the negative messages that might be in your head.

Write down your own personal coping statements below. The wording should make you feel good. It should be relevant and achievable.

Potential stressful situation   **Personal coping statement**

_____   _____

_____   _____

_____   _____

_____   _____

_____   _____

_____   _____

_____   _____

_____   _____

_____   _____

Developing a more positive thinking style can reduce our levels of stress and allow us to act more constructively and effectively.

Using these ideas to help your child

Once you discover what a difference this can make, you can use it with your child too.

- Set an example yourself with the things you say

- Let him see you responding calmly to difficult situations and people

- Encourage him to think more positively and constructively about himself and other people

- When he is expressing negative thoughts, challenge them – present him with a more accurate, positive thought.

Helping
children to
talk about
feelings

Sally was fostering six-year-old twins who had suffered emotional abuse.

'For a long time Rosie was an "angel" – so well-behaved that when I told people about her, they would say "there's no such child". But after a few months the tears started. She would be crying every two minutes and saying things about herself like "I hate myself, I'm not a nice person, I wish I was dead".

'Whenever they had had contact with their birth parents, their behaviour was always particularly challenging. When Rosie is upset I ask her to tell me about it. If I don't push too much and let her take it at her own pace, she will eventually come out with it and say: "What if they take me away from you?"

'I teach the children that they are safe with me and that they can come to me if there's anything they want to talk about.'

Looking at the changes

Think back over the ideas and suggestions you have learned about through this training programme.

When you have thought about the concepts, completed the exercises and spent some time trying out the various strategies, think about what has changed as a result.

Try to write down three things in response to each of the questions below.

The changes I have noticed

- **How have your feelings, beliefs and attitudes changed?**

  _____

  _____

  _____

- **How has your behaviour changed?**

  _____

  _____

  _____

- **How has the child's behaviour changed?**

  _____

  _____

  _____

- **How has your relationship with the child changed?**

  _____

  _____

  _____

Baseline skills	Encouraging and building self-esteem	Setting limits and providing consequences	Additional skills
Observation	Praise	Ignoring	Working with thoughts and feelings
Being clear and specific	Attending	Calm clear instructions	
ABC analysis	Choosing alternative (target) behaviour	Time-out	"I" messages
	Tangible rewards	Ground rules	
	Reward charts	Managing rule breaking	
	Token rewards	Natural consequences	
		Logical consequences	

The skills you have learned are like a tool-bag you can draw on whenever you are facing a difficult situation. You can now select strategies to address problems with the child's behaviour – see the table above.

Whatever else you do, remember to always use the tools in Column 2 – encouraging and building self-esteem. Without enough praise, rewards and positive attention, the other strategies won't work.

Setting goals for change

Decide which behaviour you are concerned about and then decide how you are going to tackle it, using one or more of the strategies you have learned. You might want to focus on one of the behaviours you identified at the beginning of this programme, which you listed on page **4**, or you might want to focus on something different.

With this behaviour in mind, work out three goals for the coming week. Be as specific as possible. For example, suppose your child is rude and aggressive when you ask him to do something. Your goals for the week might be:

Goal 1: Give clear, calm instructions

Goal 2: Ignore rude behaviour

Goal 3: Praise and reward him when he speaks to you nicely

At the end of the week, write down whether or not you achieved your goals. Make a note of what went well and what didn't go so well.

	Goal	Goal achieved? Yes/No	Comments
1			
2			
3			

Tackling problem behaviours

Remember the three problem behaviours you identified on page **4**? You may have already tackled them during the course of this programme. If not, now is the time.

You have learned new strategies and can choose which ones to use in different situations. Here's a three-week plan to follow:

- **Week 1:**
  Focus on Problem 1, setting yourself three goals each week, as you did in the exercise above.

- **Week 2:**
  Focus on Problem 2, setting three goals. Continue the approach you were using with Problem 1.

- **Week 3:**
  Focus on Problem 3, setting three goals. Continue your approach to Problems 1 and 2, adapting if necessary – for instance, if you are using a reward chart, you might want to set new targets for your child.

- **At the end of this period, rate the problem behaviours again, below.**

Mark the line at the appropriate place to indicate how severe the problem is now.

Problem 1: _____

Not a problem ←————————————————————→ Couldn't be worse

Problem 2: _____

Not a problem ←————————————————————→ Couldn't be worse

Problem 3: _____

Not a problem ←————————————————————→ Couldn't be worse

● **Now compare these ratings with the ratings you gave at the beginning of the programme, on page 4. You will be able to see just how much progress you have made with your child's most challenging behaviours.**

Caring for yourself

It's great to have new behaviour management skills, but they are not enough on their own – you also need to be psychologically strong in order to look after children who may be troubled and disturbed.

As a carer you give to others all the time: you guide and comfort them, cuddle them, keep them healthy, well fed, busy and entertained, you nurture their friendships and talents and help and support them with everything from homework to cleaning out the hamster cage. You may have to meet other people's needs too, such as those of your own parents and other family members.

It's no wonder if you sometimes feel completely drained. So it's important to spend some time on yourself – on doing the things that make you feel better, more relaxed or more energised and happier. Write down some of the things you enjoy and look forward to. It might be as simple as lying back in a bubble bath with a glossy magazine, or going for a swim (without the kids!). It might be going to a dance class or to a support group or foster carer group meeting.

You need to value yourself and make time for the things that *you* need too. Of course there will always be times when life gets in the way, but in a normal week you do need to prioritise some activities and treats that will recharge your batteries.

Write down here the time you are going to carve out for yourself in the week and what you are going to do with it.

"Me-time"	What I'm going to do with it

Don't forget – you have earned the right to have some pleasure, leisure and fun. And the more relaxed and happier you are, the better it is for your children. You need to look after yourself so you can look after them.

Well done!

Congratulations on completing this programme – we hope that you and your child or children are enjoying the benefits and will continue to do so for a long time to come.